Youth Development

From the Trenches

A Practitioner Examines the Research, His Experience, and Discovers A Powerful New Youth Development Strategy

Rick Miller

SAGAMORE
PUBLISHING

Publishers: Peter L. Bannon and Joseph J. Bannon
Director of Sales and Marketing: M. Douglas Sanders
Director of Development and Production: Susan M. Davis
Director of Technology: Christopher Thompson

ISBN print: 978-1-57167-690-0
ISBN ebook: 978-1-57167-691-7
Library of Congress Catalog Card Number: 2012934691

Sagamore Publishing, LLC
1807 N Federal Dr.
Urbana, IL 61801

http://www.sagamorepub.com

This book is dedicated to my wife, Esther,
who helped me when I was in college by reading and typing
my papers before we had computers,
and hasn't stopped since. . .

Contents

Preface

Since 1968 I have been fully committed and engaged in youth development, trying to better understand why some children do well in life and others struggle. Equal to that question was an effort to determine why some children who face many of life's greatest adversities are able to overcome great risks and experience success. Those questions guided and sustained my curiosity and enthusiasm about the development of our youth.

My first venture into the world of youth development began at age 19 as a day camp counselor for the Anaheim, California YMCA, followed by a two years as a head recreation leader with the City of Cypress, California. My first full-time employment after college was as the educational director for the Boys Club of San Gabriel Valley (now Boys & Girls Club) in El Monte, California, where I gained first-hand experience with threats such as drugs, gangs, school failure, and aimlessness—factors that greatly impact children. From El Monte, I accepted an executive director's position at a Boys Club in Buena Park, California, a challenging, low socioeconomic pocket within affluent Orange County, where many of the problems I first experienced in El Monte were also present.

In 1978, I was 30 years old, had been married for nine years to Esther, and was the proud father of Kimberly Miriam (age 8) and Aaron Joel (age 3). Encouraged by a growing interest in public policy and its effect on child and youth development, I was excited with my new job as the National Director of Government Relations for Boys & Girls Clubs of America. I wrote testimony and public policy papers, attended high level Congressional and Cabinet meetings, and spent a year on a White House committee as a loaned executive working for President Ronald Reagan's Task Force on Private Sector Initiatives, an effort designed to maximize the power of the business and voluntary sectors to minimize government's role in our lives. I testified before Congress on such issues as juvenile justice and delinquency prevention and had the honor of spending time in the oval office with President Carter as well as President Reagan.

In 1983, I accepted the job as President and Executive Director of the Boys & Girls Clubs of Metropolitan Phoenix, Arizona. This, our family's second cross-country move in five years, gave me an opportunity to return to the trenches where the real work of child and youth development takes place.

But it was in 1993 that my life's work was to be profoundly defined. I was attending a seminar where a principal of a local high school was discussing a program that had received national attention. During his presentation he shared his programs for "at-risk" students. In an odd moment he hesitated, looked unconsciously at the ceiling, allowed his eyes to return to the audience and then shared this thought, "When you think about it, all of our students are 'at risk.'"

It was as though a lightning bolt had struck me. I don't know why I felt like that considering I already knew the expression *at risk*. I used it daily to describe many of the children that my organization serves. It was a prerequisite term that had to be used in order to have any chance of securing corporate, government, United Way, or foundation funding.

So why was I taken aback by hearing the principal use that term? What actually struck me were not the words *at risk* but the fact that he used it to define all students. My practitioner and public policy experience suggested that some children and youth are indeed at risk, but claiming that all children are at risk troubled me.

I obsessed about that moment for a good number of weeks trying to better understand why a high school principal whose school had received national acclaim offered commentary that troubled my seasoned understanding about our youth. Was he right or wrong?

A few months later I was invited to attend an event held twice a year in our state called Arizona's Town Hall where a cross section of interested citizens gather at the Grand Canyon to wrestle with major issues. That year's theme was "Who is Responsible for Arizona's Children?" Certainly, it was a subject I felt qualified to discuss. One of the forum's keynote speakers was a celebrated juvenile court judge from outside our state. All that I remember from his speech was, "Today, all America's children are 'at risk.'" My fellow participants nodded in agreement with the judge's statement. I was stunned!

I resolved to challenge that claim and prove that although some children may be at risk, there was no way all children are at risk. Furthermore, maybe we had it all together wrong. Maybe all children are, in fact, *at hope*.

As I embarked on the defining journey of my career, I quickly learned that as a country we were fully invested in the at-risk paradigm. We had created an entire industry around a pervasive falsehood that was denigrating our most precious national resource. The "at-risk" industry would distract us for decades from focusing on children's assets. We would be consumed with their liabilities and deficits.

This was an arduous effort. Not only was I to battle the at-risk empire, I found many in education, child and youth development unwilling to rethink this issue.

As noted, the first 30 years of my professional career was as a practitioner. However, in 1984 I was invited to join the adjunct faculty at Arizona State University. Over the years since, I've applied my practical experience to teaching courses in voluntarism, nonprofit management, youth development—even a course entitled "Human Services for At-Risk Youth." In 1998 I was appointed ASU's first Practitioner in Residence for its newly created Center for Not for Profit Management and Leadership, now called Lodestar Center for Philanthropy and Nonprofit Innovation.

Through ASU relationships I had the opportunity to work with a range of academics whose expertise, advice, and guidance I sought in order to provide the evidence required to scientifically understand what I felt was true about children and youth–that they were *at hope* rather than *at risk*.

To test our theories, my colleagues and I read a good amount from a variety of disciplines: studies from psychology, sociology, social work, education, recreation, medicine, and criminology. In 2000, after seven years of reviewing the research, we announced at a major forum sponsored by ASU our findings and conclusions. We were excited to add our work to the ever-growing body supporting understanding of success, resiliency, failure, risk, and hope and their relationships to the fields of child and youth development.

I trust that you will be inspired, empowered, and transformed by reading this book as it offers caring adults the knowledge and skill set needed to support the success of every child.

Rick Miller

Introduction

What We Know: The Good, the Bad and the Ugly

We know much about our children today—or do we? We know their tests scores. We know how many of them drop out of school, are unemployed, in jail, commit suicide, take drugs, and become pregnant.

The following is the good, the bad and the ugly about today's children (cited from Annie E. Casey Foundation *Kids Count Data Book 2011* and State of America's Children 2011 by Children's Defense Fund). Each day in America

- 2 mothers die in childbirth,
- 5 children are killed by abuse or neglect,
- 5 children or teens commit suicide,
- 8 children or teens are killed by firearms,
- 32 children or teens die from accidents,
- 80 babies die before their first birthdays,
- 186 children are arrested for violent offenses,
- 368 children are arrested for drug offenses,
- 949 babies are born at low birth weight,
- 1,204 babies are born to teen mothers,
- 1,240 public school students are corporally punished,*
- 2,163 babies are born without health insurance,
- 2,058 children are confirmed as abused or neglected,
- 3,312 high school students drop out of school,*
- 2,573 babies are born into poverty,
- 4,133 children are arrested,
- 4,717 babies are born to unmarried mothers, and
- 18,493 public school students are suspended.

(*Based on 180 school days a year)

The following provides additional detail about children:

- More than one in eight preschool children lives with a parent who abuses or is dependent on alcohol or other drugs.

- More than 1.7 million children have a parent in prison. About 45 percent of these children are Black.

- 1,741,379 children were arrested in 2008.

- In seven states, Black juveniles are about 10 times as likely as White juveniles to be in secure residential placement (2006).

- White, Black, and Hispanic teens are equally likely to use drugs. Black teens are almost twice as likely as White teens to be arrested for drug offenses and more than five times as likely to be incarcerated for drug offenses (2006-2008).

- Forty-six percent of Black high school students, 39% of Hispanic and 11% of White students attend the 2,000 "dropout factories" across our country, where less than 60% of the freshman class graduates in four years with a regular diploma.

- One in 18 high school students reported staying home from school because they felt unsafe at school or going to or from school.

- The United States has the highest teen birth rate among comparable countries. The U.S. teen birth rate is nearly twice as high as that in the United Kingdom (26.7 per 1,000), which has the highest teen birth rate in Europe. The U.S. rate is more than triple the rate in Canada (14.1 per 1,000).

- The number of children living in families where no parent has full-time, year-round employment increased from 27% in 2008 to 31% in 2009. This increase represents 2.9 million more children living in families without secure parental employment.

- Nationwide, there was an increase of children in single-parent families, from 31% in 2000 to 34% in 2009. 3.1 million more children were living in single-parent families in 2009 than in 2000.

These are the hardcore conditions faced by our children. We have collected such statistics for many years. We had yet to directly ask our kids about how they feel about their lives. We need to understand the psychological effects of conditions we continue to document.

Fortunately, beginning in 2009-2010, the Gallup organization started surveying America's youth by asking them to share their daily experiences and how they envisioned their future. The following is from a representative sample of over 700,000 children who responded by midyear 2010:

- Half of American students are hopeful (53%). These students were found to possess numerous ideas and abundant energy for their future. Thirty-one percent said they were stuck, and 16% stated they were discouraged.

- Nearly two-thirds are engaged in school. This means they are highly involved with and enthusiastic about school, prepared, and eager to learn. Twenty-three percent note they are not engaged and are just going through the motions, and 14% admit undermining the teaching and learning process for themselves and others.

- Seventy percent feel great about their lives. They think about and plan for their future. Their health is good, relationships are sound, and basic needs are met. Thirty percent are struggling or suffering; these students seem to lack personal support and social resources.

After digesting these facts and figures, one would surely be exhausted, if not numb. How could we not be pessimistic about our children's future considering the great number of real or potential risks in their lives?

According to Albert Bandura and Martin Seligman, past presidents of the American Psychological Association, we have spent an enormous amount to time committed to studying failure rather than studying success. We agree: Studying only the risk factors as some social scientists do does not offer hope or success. It's time to look at the immunity rather than the disease.

Fortunately, the study of hope, success, and resiliency reveals a more promising story (as cited in WestEd, 2004):

A consistent yet amazing finding over the last two decades of resilience research is that most children and youth, even those from highly stressed families or resource-deprived communities, do somehow manage to make decent lives for themselves. In fact, for just about any population of children that research has found to be at greater risk than normal for later problems—children who experience divorce, live with stepparents, lose a sibling, have attention deficit disorder, suffer developmental delays, become delinquent, run away, get involved in religious cults, and so on—more of these children make it than do not (Rhodes & Brown, 1991).

In most studies, the figures seem to average 70% to 75% and include children who were placed in foster care (Festinger, 1984), were members of gangs (Vigil, 1990), were born to teen mothers (Furstenberg, 1998), had substance-abusing or mentally ill families (Beardslee, 1988; Chess, 1989; Watt, 1984; Werner, 1986; Werner & Smith 2001), and grew up in poverty (Clausen, 1993; Schweinhart et al., 1993; Vaililant, 2002).

In absolute worst-case scenarios, when children experience multiple and persistent risks, still half of them overcome adversity and achieve good developmental outcomes. (Rutter, 1987, 2000)

After reviewing these data, we wanted to better understand the following questions:

- What were the 70% to 75% of kids getting to overcome their adversities that the other 25% to 30% who were exposed to the same risk factors not receiving?

- What were 50% of the children receiving as suggested in the "worst-case scenarios" that allowed them to overcome risk that the other 50% were not getting?

Ann Masten (2009), a leading expert in the field of resiliency research and a distinguished professor at the University of Minnesota, offers the following to help us understand the difference.

Study after study has revealed a frequency list of factors associated with resilience. These "usual suspects" probably look familiar. A short list of resilience factors for children and youth includes

- effective parents and caregivers;
- connections to other competent and caring adults;
- problem-solving skills;
- self-regulation skills;
- positive beliefs about the self;
- beliefs that life has meaning;
- spirituality, faith, and religious affiliations;
- socioeconomic advantages;
- pro-social, competent peers and friends;
- effective teachers and schools; and
- safe and effective communities.

This short list came from research on young people, but research on adults suggests that many of these same resilience factors continue to be important (sometimes in more mature forms), as people grow older. Close relationships, for example, are important across the lifespan, first with parents and later with friends or romantic partners. This list provides important clues to what matters for resilience, leading me to conclude that there must be fundamental protective systems for human resilience.

Some examples of basic protective systems for human resilience include

- attachment relationships,
- human intelligence and information processing (a human brain in good working order),
- motivation to adapt and opportunities for agency (mastery motivation),

- self-control and emotion regulation (self-regulation),
- religious and cultural systems that nurture human development and resilience, and
- schools and communities that nurture and support human development and resilience.

What are we to learn from this? What youth are telling us is "You can mess all you want with instruction, curriculum, policy, and program strategies, and while all that is important, it doesn't substitute for the basics. We need adults who care about us as people and believe in us when no one else does, even when we don't seem to care about ourselves. Make sure we are connected to family, school, and community, and help us to see that education is relevant to our lives. In return, we will be better students, achieve our potential, and feel that life is an exciting journey."

The idea of studying what we actually need to know is not new to science. It's just that from time to time it appears we get lost in our journey. For example, I am reminded of a young British country physician who in the late 1700s noticed that milkmaids who suffered from cowpox appeared to be resistant to smallpox. This seemingly modest observation led to the discovery of the smallpox vaccine. Less than 100 years later, the World Heath Organization announced that this terrible disease, which had claimed over 300 million lives in the 20th century alone, had been eradicated. The lesson learned: *Don't study only the disease; also study the immunity.*

In his book, *One Small Step Can Change Your Life*, Robert Maurer, associate clinical professor at the UCLA School of Medicine, also reminds us about missing simple answers because the problems seem so great. He offers this story to make his point:

Many Americans are unaware that diarrhea kills a million children around the world each year. To put this number into perspective, that's the equivalent of a jumbo jet full of children crashing every four hours. Global health-care experts and governmental organizations have attempted to reduce this occurrence through large scale, costly solutions, such as delivering improved plumbing systems to the beleaguered areas or introducing oral rehydration therapy to the medical facilities that serve these children. These efforts are laudable and useful, but they demonstrate blindness to one very small problem that leads to diarrhea: dirty hands. In the countries where fatal childhood diarrhea is most prevalent, soap is usually present in the house, but only 15 to 20% of people use it before handling food or babies. When people keep their hands clean, diarrhea cases can be reduced by more than 40%. It is easier to teach a person to prevent diarrhea by washing his or her hands than it is to install new plumbing across a continent or to supply a therapy after the disease has taken hold. (pp. 135-136)

The following chapters outline the remarkable body of work, conclusions, principles, and practices found to dramatically help all young people achieve productive and satisfying lives. Be prepared—it may be much simpler than you would expect.

Chapter One

Challenging Conventional Wisdom

Many people fall victim to conventional wisdom. In the child and youth development and education fields, conventional wisdom clearly holds that some children will do very well, others average, and—inevitably—some will fail. Over time we have institutionalized that conventional wisdom without fully challenging it. Just look around. We have programs for young people who do extremely well, others for our average children, and many systems for youth who struggle to find a positive place in society.

Our school grading systems consist of As, Bs, Cs, Ds, and Fs, or Excellent, Satisfactory, Unsatisfactory, or Needs Improvement. These systems are in place because we expect students to earn these grades.

Youth-serving organizations continue to design and develop disciplinary protocols. History tells that children have issues requiring these programs. Society is even prepared for youth who break laws. We expect to lock some of them up.

Based on conventional wisdom, we have created a great number of programs to prevent developmentally detrimental behavior. For example, if there is a drug problem, we create a drug prevention program. If we sense a gang problem it would be prudent to create a gang prevention service. If it is determined there is a school drop-out issue, that would, of course, require a school drop-out prevention program. The same pattern would occur if we were worried about bullying, teen pregnancy, and/or alcohol abuse. These prevention and/or intervention programs could go on endlessly. Find a problem, create a program; find another problem, add another program. Let's continue that process until we finally realize that

- children who succeed in life do so when we focus on their assets, not their liabilities;

- programs don't make a difference in children's lives, relationships do; and

- children grow up holistically and are the sum total of all their experiences, not just one institution's service or activity.

If that is the case, what's a community, school, or organization to do? It begins by challenging conventional wisdom.

Professor Albert Einstein gave us a clue to this dilemma when he said, "We cannot solve today's significant problems at the same level of thinking we were at when we created them." Einstein's assessment is clear: It's time to challenge what we think we know. Unless we do so, we will continue to see the types of statistics collected by the Annie E. Casey Foundation, the Children's Defense Fund, the Gallup Student Poll, and others.

Over the centuries, our greatest achievements have resulted from changing the way we think. Beyond the obvious inventions in technology or other discoveries in medicine, society has been most transformed simply by thoughts.

Such powerful thoughts were written by a freckle-faced, six-foot-two, red haired, 33-year-old attorney who spent two and half weeks in a boarding house in Philadelphia, just thinking. He captured his ideas in this expression: "We hold these truths to be self-evident, that all men are created equal. They are endowed by their Creator with certain inalienable rights; that among these are life, liberty, and the pursuit of happiness." That idea was powerful enough to spawn a new nation (Thomas Jefferson, 1776).

One hundred ninety-two years later and only 200 miles from Philadelphia, a 34-year-old minister addressed more than 100,000 people with a commanding new idea, a new way of thinking: " . . . my four little children will one day live in a nation where they will not be judged by the color of their skin, but by the content of their character" (Martin Luther King, 1963). These words thoughtfully and beautifully defined a civil rights struggle by simply and powerfully envisioning a new future for our country.

If we can change the course of history with great ideas, is it not time to suggest that "All children are capable of success, no exceptions?" Conventional wisdom is conventional only as long as it isn't challenged.

Each chapter in this book examines the dynamics of risk and—most importantly—the power of hope. We explore whether risk and hope are actually manifestations of the same thing. We seek to understand whether eliminating risk offers hope to our children. We redefine words such as *success, future,* and *potential* because they are part of conventional wisdom. We challenge well-meaning programs along with established bureaucracies while exploring a culture.

And, if that is not enough conventional wisdom to challenge, we suggest a new discipline of study within our institutions of higher learning: *Hopeology*.

Hopeology sounds odd, but not so much when further examined. Over the years, various groups have determined which disciplines require greater study. Most colleges and universities offer degrees in widely ranging areas and specializations within many. Criminology, for instance, might include the dynamics of crime, its history, root causes, prevention, intervention, and punishment theories and practices. Advanced studies may examine why some countries consider some behaviors criminal and others don't, or why some behavior is criminal only past a certain age threshold.

We are not suggesting that crime is not an important area of study. However, I would suggest that if crime is so important to study, why not also study hope? Isn't it hope that gives reason to life—to try, to achieve, to not give up, to be happy, healthy, and courageous? Doesn't hope deserve its own discipline? Could such an idea challenge conventional wisdom?

What is hope? We all have some understanding of what it feels like to have high hopes, a little, or none. Even apart from a faith-based definition of hope, hope relates to goals and energy, dreaming and realizing one's dreams. Where does that come from? Is there a hope gene? Could hope be taught like reading, math, tying one's shoes, or driving a car? Can one learn or receive hope only from a hopeful person such as parents? Might a hope vaccine provide immunity from the ravages of hopelessness, pessimism, and failure?

These questions and hundreds more need study, testing, and answers. Our goal is clear: Understanding why some children do well and others struggle cannot come from conventional means.

In this quest to challenge conventional wisdom, we also challenge the conventional methods we use to support youth. Instead of delivering a series of well-meaning programs or services to youth, we instead offer our findings within a *strategic cultural framework*.

A what? Yes, a strategic cultural framework!

Chapter Two

Remembering the Pygmalion Effect

Remember the Pygmalion effect? The consequences of Rosenthal and Jacobson's landmark study, "Pygmalion in the Classroom" (1968), are still relevant. What we learned from the study and must remember is that adults' attitudes—not just their qualifications, credentials, experiences, and skills—influence a child's development. The "self-fulfilling prophecy" theory is as true today as ever.

I recall a conversation with a schoolteacher friend. The discussion was focused on the broad subject of expectations in education. That theme took us to the issue of labeling children. My friend, a 20-year public school system professional, proudly noted that within the first two weeks of a new school year, she could predict which students would do well and which would struggle. My first reaction was, "Well, that makes sense." After all those years in the classroom, teaching thousands of children, one would think that a seasoned educator would be in a position to make such an assertion. After further thought, the danger in such predicting became clear, especially if it cast a student in a negative light. It seems reckless to judge children in just two weeks with expectations that could seal their fate.

Teachers, youth workers, school bus drivers, parents, school custodians, food service workers, community volunteers—everyone who helps in raising children—needs to be aware of the impact of expectations.

Such predicting is played out every day—sometimes in the child's favor, sometimes to a definite loss. We must be vigilant in monitoring our words and thoughts, especially when we present children in ways that could be detrimental to their development.

This lesson was reinforced during a youth development class I was teaching at Arizona State University. We were discussing the many ways adults label children. Most labels are offered without thinking about the consequences: words such as *good, bad, smart, learning disabled, at risk, hoodlum, gangbanger, nerd,* and *lazy.*

One student shared a story about working as an intern with a state agency responsible for transporting juveniles who had been arrested from jail to a group home or other appropriate facility. She noted that prior to taking my class and understanding the power of the self-fulfilling prophecy, she would automatically label consciously and unconsciously these wards of the court as hoodlums. She felt they deserved no respect from her other than to transport them from one destination to another.

One evening she was driving a 15-year-old girl from lock up to a group home. The girl had been arrested for shoplifting. This particular evening, she struck up a conversation with the frightened teen. She learned that the young lady's father had abandoned her when she was an infant, that her mother was disabled, and in addition to going to school, the teenager was responsible for four younger siblings. My student's preconceptions were shattered. She now saw a girl overcoming great obstacles and still surviving. "You have tremendous potential and strength," she told the girl. Before getting out of the car, the teen thanked my student and said she hoped one day to help kids like herself make better decisions. This was as simple act of kindness between a caring adult and a frightened kid.

So why are we so quick to label kids? According to Robert Tauber (1998), it's almost impossible not to form conclusions even with very little information about a child. As a matter of fact, human beings need to form conclusions based on cause and effect. In education and youth development, we tend to assign factors as to why children behave or perform academically the way they do. We draw upon our own experiences and those of others. Regardless of how we come to those conclusions, we sometimes find ourselves correct and other times we are in great error.

We hear descriptors of youth in general—they are *lazy, rebellious, lack interest or ability,* are *mean spirited, have bad parents,* etc. In addition to understanding how our perceptions—right or wrong—affect children, we need to learn strategies that might tilt the pendulum in their favor.

An interesting study entitled *Attribution Versus Persuasion as a Means for Modifying Behavior* (Miller, Brickman, & Bolen, 1975), followed a group of fifth graders, observing how tidy and neat they were in keeping their classroom clean. Similar to the Pygmalion Effect (Self-Fulfilling Prophecy), the study assessed attribution theory. Sharma (1998) and Tripathi (1995) suggest that "attributions by teachers for students' performance are very effective in changing students' behavior." These researchers shared wrapped candy with the class. They then counted the number of candy wrappers thrown on the floor or put in the trash. This activity took place over several weeks. As would be expected in the early part of the experiment, there were many more wrappers on the floor than the trash. The fifth graders were divided into two groups. The attribution group was repeatedly told over a period of time how neat and tidy they were. Their teacher, principal, and custodian shared these messages. The other group was the persuasion group, (i.e., the more common approach to changing behavior); this group was told the importance of being neat and tidy. The control group received no treatment.

The attribution group significantly changed the children's behavior related to being neat and tidy. The researchers then studied the same influences to determine their effect on school performance, namely in math by second graders. Again, the attribution group math scores improved over the persuasion and control groups' performances.

It's obvious that we are most effective when we intentionally and intrinsically reinforce children's self-image and connect that to a desired behavior than we are when we externally try to control them by persuasion or power of position, (i.e., "clean up the room because I told you so.").

The children in these studies came to understand that neatness and good math performance were due to how they saw themselves. And how they saw themselves was due to how adults perceived them. The Pygmalion Theory reveals the power of adult attitudes and their affect on youth. When adults use that understanding in a positive way by attributing positive traits to children, children's behavior and performance improve.

Below are two examples of statements offered in the neat and tidy study used by the researchers that relate to attribution theory:

- "My, this is a neat classroom. You must be very neat students who care about how their room looks," offered by the principal.

- "This is the neatest class in school. You must be very neat and clean students," written on the chalkboard by the custodian.

- The classroom teacher offered similar statements.

Here are statements used to introduce attribution concepts to the children related to math performance:

- "You seem to know your arithmetic assignments very well."

- "You really work hard in math."

- "You're trying more; keep at it!"

Here is how persuasion training attempts to influence behavior:

- "You should be good at math."

- "You should be getting better grades in math."

- "You should be doing well in math."

The researchers found that reinforcement training was also effective. In this regard, teachers would say or write to the student:

- "I'm proud of your work."

- "I'm pleased with your progress."

- "Excellent progress."

I learned first hand about the power of both of these theories and practices while serving as executive director of the Boys & Girls Clubs of Buena Park, California.

The Story of Santos

It was a beautiful spring day in southern California and a very busy one for the Boys & Girls Club; it was the United Way's annual visit to our agency. Their purpose was to review our efforts and effectiveness in order to determine if we deserved an allocation increase.

It's a day when you share the best of who you are and what you do. It's like having company coming, and you take special care in making sure your home is "spic and span" so your guests will think that you live that way all the time. Everything in our club was refreshed. The floors were buffed, shelves were dusted, bulletin boards were current, interesting, and artistic, and the staff looked professional in their matching polo shirts.

We also had a series of staff meetings in anticipation of the visit. Those meetings included discussions about some of our more challenging youth. We wanted to make sure the United Way understood that some of the young people we serve are usually not welcome by other organizations.

I wanted our community to understand what made our Boys & Girls Club unique. A large part of that uniqueness had to do with the types of children we reached.

One group of children we served just needed a safe place to go after school, weekends, vacations, and holidays and didn't need a serious prevention or intervention program—they were doing well. They just needed safety, security, and enjoyment.

Second, we served children who were challenged by their environment and sometimes by themselves. They appeared to be at a crossroads in life. They were being pulled in two different directions—one negative, one positive. Gangs, school drop out, poor social skills, aggression, and apathy were forces affecting them. The club was to be a counter force. Our club was a place where they could receive the guidance they needed. We wanted them to know there were negative forces in their lives but there were also positive opportunities.

The third category included kids who needed a second, third, fourth, or fifth chance. They had reputations that usually came with some type of record, whether it was from the school, law enforcement, or the community. These youth were usually not welcomed by many groups. The club was a wholesome environment for them. Each day it was a fresh start if they wanted and respected it—a new day to write a more positive chapter in their life. But make no mistake, if that wasn't the reason they were coming to the club, they would be asked to leave but would be welcomed back again to give it another try. In other words, we didn't give up on kids.

Then there was Santos. Just when I figured out how to label kids and put them in the right categories, along came a young person who would challenge everything I thought I knew about youth.

Santos defied a straightforward description. Suffice it to say he was one of the meanest and most ornery children in our community. Good days at the club were days when Santos was absent. Bad days were those when he showed up at our facility. And there are days regardless of bad or good behavior that you just didn't feel it would be in anybody's interest to have Santos present. The United Way's annual visit was one of those days.

As luck would have it, it was exactly that time when Santos, after not visiting the Club for a few days, decided to show up. It did not take long to be aware that Santos was in our facility. Kids were screaming as Santos made his rounds, slapping them on the back of the head. He walked into the arts and crafts room and messed up the paintings and sculptures painstakingly created by members. He walked into the gym, grabbed a basketball during a game, and tossed it into the street. Yes, Santos was in the club.

There was no time to think, only to react. The United Way group was to arrive in 90 minutes. I could not take any chances; I had to get Santos out of the club.

Fortunately, Santos was either afraid of or respected me; at that moment, it did not matter which. I grabbed him by the arm and said, "Come on, Santos; we are going for a ride." It was quick and precise. He was in my car and we were driving to his home.

We walked up the three steps to the front door. I stayed outside while Santos went in to get his mother to come talk to me. A few moments later, Santos' mother appeared on the other side of the screen door that separated us. It was obvious that she was not pleased to see me; I felt the same about her. She asked not so politely, "What do you want?"

Before I answered, I was overcome by a strange sensation. It was as though time stood still. I heard the question, but I was not yet prepared to answer it. I was frozen in thought. "What did I want?" That was Santos' mother's question. Why was I there? During that odd moment, flashes went through my mind. I thought of all the other adults with some authority standing on this same front porch, looking through the same screen door with Santos' mother looking from the other direction probably asking the same question: "What do you want?" My guess was school counselors, social workers, probation officers, police officers, principals, and Boys & Girls Club directors had all stood on that front porch peering through the screen door with Santos' mother gazing back.

I was sure she had heard it all before. She knew she had the rottenest kid in the city. Professionals had told her that time and again. So what was I doing there?

I returned to the moment at hand. It was time to make a difference in a child's life. What would I say or do? I had to come up with something different from all the others who preceded me on that front porch.

"Hello, my name is Rick Miller, and I am the director of the Boys & Girls Club." What was to follow would change Santos' and his family's life. "I just wanted to come by and meet you and tell you what a wonderful son you have." This is the Pygmalion and attribution theory wrapped up in one statement and moment. Santos' mother's eyes went from peering to opening as wide as saucers.

Four miracles took place on the front porch that afternoon. Miracle one—the screen door was opened, literally and symbolically, and I was invited in to speak to Santos and his parents. Miracle two—Santos' parents became two of the best volunteers the club ever had. They were now part of the community rather than apart from the community. Miracle three—I went home with two dozen of the best tamales I ever tasted. And miracle four—No Hollywood ending; Santos did not graduate from Harvard medical school. But he did graduate from high school, and I am sure no one, including me, had thought such an achievement possible.

This story has reminded me for decades of the impact and power adult attitudes have over children's futures. Once Santos understood that someone saw something special in him and was willing to go the extra mile, he became a kid at hope.

Chapter Three

Universal Truth I

Missions Versus Beliefs

Promoting a strategic cultural framework instead of a program is a great challenge. We know programs. We offer thousands of programs every day to every segment within child and youth development and education systems.

Children have much to learn and little time to prepare to be contributing members of society. What is a contributing member of society? It is an informed voter, good family person/husband or wife, a wage earner who pays a fair share of taxes, doesn't park the car on the lawn, keeps his neighborhood clean, is spiritual and honest, and doesn't speed on the open highway. . . . As the list grows, the next question is "What do children need to know to become contributing members of society?"

These lists beg for programs to teach skills in character education, academia, civic education, athletics, social recreation, arts, drama, hunting, fishing, gang prevention, drug prevention, community service, Bible study, environmental awareness, health, career exploration, home economics, public speaking, law awareness, driver education, hygiene—anything any group can conceive that purports to offer youth something they'll need now and in the future.

The end result of this exercise is myriad disjointed programs and classes disconnected from one another that somehow are expected to magically produce a productive, contributing member of society.

Unfortunately, it is not working. To repeat a few sad statistics, we have a national school drop-out rate of 28%; 42% for Hispanics; and 43% for African Americans (Education Week and the Editorial Projectes in Education Research Center, June 2011). The JFA Institute in its report, *Unlocking America* (November, 2007) stated that one-third of all African American males will be in the correction system during their lifetime. Additionally, on any given day, over 80,000 kids are in lock up in the U.S. (Office of Juvenile Justice and Deliquency Prevention, 2010). Finally, 4,000 children die from suicide every year; it is the third leading cause of death of youth ages 15-24 and the sixth leading cause of death for children, ages 5-14 (American Academy of Child and Adolescent Psychiatry, 2008). These are just a few of the appalling indicators that cry out for attention. Kids are growing up without hope!

So what's missing? Certainly not good intentions! Conventional answers do not offer us the answer, only more programs on top of more programs. Our answers are found by investigating the dynamics of what truly influences a child's development.

Our conclusion is that children do not grow up in programs or institutions; they are the sum total of all their experiences. Children grow up holistically. They grow up in cultures.

Once we acknowledge that fact, we begin to think much differently about youth and what we can do together. That is a very different strategy from our current approach of retreating to our program silos. It requires us to think culturally about what children and youth need from all of us, rather than just some of us.

What, then, is meant by culture? According to E.B. Taylor, the 18th century English anthropologist credited for defining culture, it is "that complex whole which includes knowledge, belief, art, morale, laws, custom and any other capabilities and habits as acquired by man as a member of society."

The field of cultural psychology expands   Taylor's definition of culture to include both what people do and what they think, by offering order to what would otherwise be a chaotic system, and to implicitly agree to co-construct a shared morality. (Lee & Johnson, 2007).

The word *culture* is important because it includes everything that defines what we do educationally, morally, spiritually, and ethically—and why. It defines how all of us can live, grow, and work together. Furthermore, it suggests an agreed-upon strategy to achieve our mutual goals. Therefore, the study of culture and how to use it to benefit all children and youth is critical to any child and youth development strategy.

Culture doesn't require us to abandon the need for programs, but to frame programs holistically to ensure that the sum of their parts actually equals the whole of a child. To create culture, we begin with its basic building blocks and how a child and youth development strategy can be defined by it.

The first building block in creating a culture is a shared belief. This is where we need to distinguish and differentiate mission and belief statements.

We know mission statements! For decades, every institution, department, organization, and group had to have a mission statement. We have spent countless hours writing, editing, and word-smithing to death our mission statements. No sooner is a mission statement completed than it is time to rewrite it. Yet, experience suggests that only those who wrote the mission statement can define it. Most employees, clients, or customers of the organization have little or no knowledge of the statement, much less of its precise wording.

Why then have them? For one reason and one reason only—to ensure that we are unique in what we do. Heaven forbid we should ever confuse Boys & Girls Clubs with the YMCA, or one school district with another. We need to know that Boy Scouts and Girl Scouts are different, whereas Big Brothers and Big Sisters are the same organization.

Have our child and youth development organizations become so specialized that we have forgotten that children do not grow up in only one organization or program, but are the sum total of all their experiences? Children grow up holistically, so why do we insist on dividing and conquering child development? Instead, why don't we encourage these disconnected and fragmented services to share a common culture?

Rather than having unique mission statements, we could share the concept that "All children are capable of success, no exceptions!" Those who accept this statement can create a culture; those who don't—well, we may need to move forward without them.

Whether teaching a class at Arizona State University, guest lecturing on college campuses across the country, or facilitating workshops, seminars, and institutes, I spend a significant amount of time examining the important difference between mission statements and belief statements: *Mission statements are owned; belief statements are shared.* Creating an organization or program requires a mission statement. Creating a culture requires a belief statement.

This distinction is critical because it strikes at the core of child and youth development and education systems. If we wish to fragment and disconnect these systems, thus jeopardizing the holistic development of children, then we should continue to create missions without regard to what we need to share about the development of children. If we see instead the critical need to address child and youth development more comprehensively, it may be time to explore and introduce a shared belief statement.

To emphasize this point during my lectures, I ask, "Why is it we call our country the United States of America?" Interesting question? I think so, and I try to convince my students of its unique value. Why don't we call our country the "Federated States of America," or the "Independent States of America" or just the "States of America"? In fact, what is it that actually unites us? Is it our geography? Hawaii and Alaska are not contiguous. Could it be our religion? Socio-economic status? Politics? If all of those factors divide us, then how do we have the audacity to claim to be the *United* States of America?

Simply and powerfully, it is the belief statement offered in our Declaration of Independence: "We hold these truths to be self-evident, that all men are created equal, they are endowed by their creator with certain inalienable rights, that among them are life, liberty, and the pursuit of happiness." That is a shared belief; and even in a country so politically, socially, economically, religiously, geographically, racially, and ethnically diverse, it offers us the power to be united. Perhaps they were on to something in the 1700s.

What we learned by sharing a belief statement to unite rather than a mission statement to divide is the understanding that we are much stronger, more able, and certainly more effective together than we can ever be alone.

Within our massive child and youth development and education systems, we must be willing to explore something important enough that we are willing to suspend our self-interests without abandoning our missions for something greater than any one group or sector can achieve alone.

The answer to what that is comes straight from a review of the literature and forms the basis for the first of three powerful findings we call Universal Truths. They are found throughout research studies and apply equally to all youth.

Universal Truth I

*Children succeed when surrounded by adults
who believe they will succeed.*

The magnitude of that statement ushers in the first cultural building block where every child is seen as capable of success, no exceptions. The statement does not create a new organization or program, but an inclusive participatory culture.

Chapter Four

Testing Our Beliefs by Checking Our Blood Pressure

We have our first Universal Truth expressed: *Children succeed when surrounded by adults who believe they will succeed.* This belief serves as the foundation to our cultural framework.

Whereas a mission statement establishes the reason an organization exists, a belief statement is both personal and shared. This first Universal Truth is derived from understanding that children have a greater chance to succeed when surrounded by adults who believe they will succeed. We interpret that finding as *all children are capable of success, no exceptions.*

The challenge is how do we know if the adults working with children believe in them?

For example, if medical science reports normal blood pressure is 120 over 80, we test our blood pressure against that norm. If we don't, we take the risk of assuming we have normal blood pressure without really knowing if we do. If our actual blood pressure is 160 over 100, we may be in jeopardy of a stroke, hypertension, or a heart attack. The same holds true about our beliefs in children. The science is very clear: Children have a greater chance of growing up hopeful, optimistic, and successful if surrounded by adults who believe in their capacity to succeed. Knowing that requires us to examine whether we are surrounding children with adults who believe they can succeed.

To discover whether adults working with children believe in them, we created an 11-question survey called Culture Scan. A Likert Scale beginning with "1" (*strongly disagree*) to "10" (*strongly agree*) captures the responses to the statement. To date, we have surveyed more than 1,000 adults who are either on the front lines working with children or are in a support role. The first question in our survey is "Do you believe all children are capable of success, no matter what?"

In this survey, "normal blood pressure" is a 10. Anything less threatens the future for many students. So how do we fare? Unfortunately, only 53% of our respondents are able to select the number 10. That leaves 47% choosing a number less than 10. Remember that children do much better and are more likely to experience success when surrounded by adults who believe in their capacity to succeed. The survey reports that 47% of people working with children, directly or indirectly, are unable to strongly agree with the statement.

To put this finding in perspective, what would we do if we found 47% of a group of patients to be outside the range of what we know is a normal blood pressure reading? Certainly, we would expect some intervention: diet, exercise, meditation, or drug therapy, because it would not be prudent to ignore the threat.

Before discussing our prescribed intervention related to the findings and their importance to children's academic, emotional, and social health, let's investigate the primary reason why so many adults who work with children find it difficult to believe that *all children are capable of success, no matter what.*

When interviewed, adults who selected a number less than 10 on the Likert Scale most commonly offered reasons having to do with "reality." We were told that there are too many examples of children not succeeding, with the risk factors discussed earlier including but not limited to dysfunctional families, abusive and or neglectful parents, apathy about education, poor neighborhoods, differing value systems, language hurdles, and educational barriers.

We learned from these interviews that self-proclaimed realists may never be able to circle number 10, primarily because they are realists. Realists are individuals who predict the future based on their observations of the past and the present. That is why they are realists. They know what is going to happen before it happens. After reviewing the challenging statistics about the condition of today's youth, it would be easy to agree with those who point to those findings as reasons some children might not succeed.

In interviewing respondents who circled 10 (*strongly agree*) we found a different trait: These people are very forward thinking, imaginative, and tenacious in their beliefs. We call them *geniuses* in contrast to *realists*. Geniuses see a world that doesn't currently exist and are willing to create that world.

In Chapter 18 we share the 11-question survey along with a case study. For now, we offer a personal story to illustrate the distinction between a realist and a genius.

I'm Married To a Realist: My Grandson Can Fly

I understand the thinking of realists inasmuch as I have been married to one for more than four decades. I did not know my wife was a realist until one pleasant Arizona day we were babysitting our then-three-year-old grandson, Jakob. Jakob had just watched the much-loved story of Peter

Pan. And, of course, after viewing Peter Pan's escapades for 90 exciting minutes, he got on top of our sofa and yelled, "Grandma, watch me fly!"

A protective and panicky grandma in her best realist voice hollered back, "Don't jump! You're going to hurt yourself."

Some of you may have anticipated my wife's admonition with your own expressions: "Don't jump! You'll break your leg, your arm, your head," or something just as bad. In other words, realists cannot contain themselves. Again, based on past and present experiences they know before something happens what's going to occur.

After hearing Grandma's well-meaning, frantic warning, our grandson nonetheless ignored her words and subsequently did what Mother Nature expected of him. He jumped, landed safely on the floor, raised his arms, and looked into his grandma's startled eyes, and said, "Grandma, it feels so good to fly!"

What my grandson was trying to convey is that sometimes it's permissible to challenge reality and not succumb to it. What I learned from witnessing this episode was the difference between being a realist and a genius. I understood what my grandson was doing. He wasn't being disrespectful or disobedient but he was literally testing the truth of reality. My grandson was allowing the genius in him to escape.

In so doing, he may someday draw upon that experience and although he learns he cannot personally fly he may, like Orville and Wilbur Wright, find a way *to* fly. That is the difference between a realist and a genius: Realists accept the fact that they cannot fly, so why even try? A genius, however, understands there may be thousands of other options available *to* fly.

You'll never hear a child identify himself or herself as a realist. That seems to be an adult onset disease. But you'll hear many adults proudly proclaim being a realist if they don't believe something can be achieved.

The following is another illustration to further distinguish between a realist and a genius.

Geniuses Don't Give Up

Thomas Edison, one our greatest inventors, was known for his tenacity. My guess is that if Mr. Edison were a realist, he would have found thousands of reasons to give up, considering the number of attempts it took him to achieve success. Depending on the reporting source, Edison made 1,000 to 5,000 attempts before successfully inventing the light bulb. Geniuses do not give up.

Applying these stories to our *Culture Scan Survey,* we are attempting to understand whether or not our children are at least given the benefit of the doubt. Are they surrounded by adults who believe that they can all succeed, No Exceptions? Those who circle 10 also understand that geniuses don't give up. Realists by definition must give up or may not even try if they don't believe something will work.

This discussion returns us to where we started. We must not give up on children. It is too easy to be a realist. We have the potential, if we wish, to circle the number 10. We shouldn't be defining children's future on what has transpired in their past.

Our cultural commitment, supported by Universal Truth I, requires a world where every child is surrounded by adults who believe in all of them and are fully committed to finding ways for all children to succeed, no exceptions.

It's equally important to recognize that conceding to *at risk* as a reason some children cannot succeed sentences them to a future where failure could define them. It is unimaginable that any adult would consciously do that. Unconsciously, though, that is exactly what is happening.

Chapter Five

Universal Truth II
The Aces

Universal Truth II states that *children succeed when they have meaningful and sustainable relationships with caring adults.* This truth, like Universal Truth I, was found throughout our literature review. It relates to success and failure regardless of the risk factors in a child's life.

Universal Truth II, simply stated, is all about relationships. But we go beyond what was commonly understood about the importance of children and youth connecting to adults. It is more than just having good parents, teachers, leaders, mentors, and role models. Those titles do not identify what happens between adult and child that makes a positive difference.

Our studies and subsequent discussion led us to identifying the four most prominent, meaningful, and sustainable components children and youth need in order to feel anchored, valued, useful, competent, remarkable, talented, and capable of success.

The most prominent and sustainable relationships and components are

- anchor parents,

- other caring adults,

- high expectations, and

- opportunities to succeed.

What was revealed were the types of relationships and components that children need. The most obvious relationship, the anchor parent(s), the unique, unconditional love that exists 24 hours a day, 365 days a year, year after year, and supports a child's physical and emotional well-being. Life is off to a great start. The absence of this critical relationship does not necessarily mean a life destined for failure, but it does suggest that life might be rockier than otherwise.

The second type of relationship identified, other caring adults, includes uncles, aunts, grandparents, teachers, youth leaders, school bus drivers, custodians, police officers, and others. This category has less to do with what is written on their business cards than what is written on their hearts. Sociologists, social workers, psychologists, and criminologists define these types of relationships as protective factors. These adults seem to protect children by mitigating their pursuit of risk, especially in behavior that could be physically and emotionally harmful.

For example, children who repeatedly skip school, get stoned, or pursue criminal behavior might feel that no one really cares about them and no one would be disappointed to learn of their reckless behavior. Children who sense that adults are concerned about their well-being are likely to want to please them.

High expectations defines those unique adults who judge children by their potential not just by their behavior. This is not easy to achieve! Most adults judge children by what they can see. It takes an exceptional person who can look beneath the surface to identify the treasures buried in youth. High expectations also means believing in children more than they believe in themselves.

Opportunities to succeed involve adults who create age-, ability-, and interest-appropriate tasks for children to experience. This includes allowing children to also define success.

These four types of relationships illustrate the metaphor of the cards one is dealt in life. Some people seem to get dealt good cards. The best four cards one could be dealt in life are the aces:

- **The Ace of Hearts** represents the anchor parent. The heart symbolizes the unconditional love we all need, especially from our parents as we grow up.

- **The Ace of Clubs** represents other caring adults. The Club is distinguished by a group of cloves. This grouping represents all the caring adults children need in their lives.

- **The Ace of Spades** points upward as a symbol for high expectations. A spade is also a shovel that can uncover treasures buried in our children.

- **The Ace of Diamonds** represents opportunities to succeed. Youth development professionals recognize that successful experiences are made up of the senses of belonging, competency, usefulness/value, and empowerment—the four points of a diamond.

Our metaphor is almost complete. The most valuable cards in a deck are the four Aces, which are used to represent the types of relationships with adults that children need. The next question is obvious: Who controls the Aces that children need to support their development? The answer is also obvious—adults do. If children are fortunate enough to be dealt all four Aces, it is because adults offer those relationships. If they receive three, two, one, or none, it is again because adults make those choices. Children don't.

Our sampling of adults working in some schools and youth groups revealed that 48% estimate that most children they serve do not receive Aces. The primarily reason may be that we are not focused on creating relationships as much as committed to delivering programs and curriculum.

Schools and youth-serving organizations track registration, attendance, and participation in programs. Excused and unexcused absences, disciplinary referrals, grades, and test scores in many cases are also tracked. We also know how many children eat in the cafeteria each day and how many ride the school bus.

Do we know, however, which students receive Aces and which students don't? According to our findings and that of others, children and youth are more successful when they feel connected in meaningful ways with caring adults. Programs, curriculum or disciplinary protocols don't make a difference—relationships do. We have tried unsuccessfully to substitute programs, instruction, and protocols for the meaningful relationships children actually need. Only when a significant relationship is struck can real learning and development take place. Why don't we assign the same importance to determining if our children are connected with caring adults as to whether they are in attendance?

Margaret Mead, the great anthropologist, identifies the importance of feeling connected: "Having someone wonder where you are when you don't come home at night is a very old human need." Professor Mead's admonition also holds true if you aren't at the bus stop, in class, or participating in a program.

We expand on Professor's Mead insight with additional quotes that strongly support the case for Aces:

- "No significant learning happens without a significant relationship," (James Comer, lecture given at Education Services Center, Region IV, Houston, TX, 1995).

- "Locate a resilient kid and you will find a caring adult, or several who have guided him" (Shapiro, et al., 1996).

- "A successful relationship occurs when emotional deposits are made to the student and emotional withdraws are avoided," (Stephen Covey, 1989).

By understanding the critical importance of giving and receiving Aces, we also recognize the need for uniform criteria that indicate when an Ace is actually given.

The Ace of Hearts can be given by those responsible for a child's physical and emotional well-being 24 hours a day, seven days a week, 365 days a year. Ideally, this is a child's parent, but may be the child's official guardian. However, parents and guardians do not automatically deal the Ace of Hearts. This Ace must be given in unconditional love.

Any caring adult who meets the following criteria may deal the Ace of Clubs:

- You have known the child/youth for at least eight weeks.
- You can describe at least three very positive characteristics/skills or talents you believe this child possesses.

- You believe this child feels comfortable asking for your assistance.

The Ace of Spades is achieved if the following criteria are met:

- You have known this child/youth for at least eight weeks.

- You believe in this child/youth even more than he/she sometimes believes in her- /himself.

- You sense that you are one of the "go-to" adults this child may contact to discuss a problem/concern beyond an academic/program issue.

- You have a very good sense of this child's/youth's experiences during the nonschool or program hours.

- You feel able to judge this student by his/her potential, not just by her/his behavior.

One other way we have come to describe the Ace of Spades is by one's ability to assess children not just by behavior, but more importantly by their potential.

The Ace of Diamonds is dealt if the following are true:

- You give this child appropriate tasks and acknowledge her/his successes.

- This child has a sense of achievement and feels valued and appreciated when in your presence.

- This child succeeds in your classroom or program/
  organization by sensing she/he belongs; feels competent,
  valued, and useful; and recognizes that his/her
  achievements offer personal empowerment.

With these defined criteria, we can track the types of
relationships children do or do not have. We can track the
intentionality of our priorities rather than just assuming
such relationships are being struck. We can determine
if these important relationships are organic or must be
achieved through other strategies.

The important commitment required is that *no* children
leave a school or program without knowing specifically
whether or not they have a meaningful and sustainable
relationship with caring adults.

Too many children grow up disconnected; some are
even anonymous. We are too focused on enrolling them in
programs and classes and less concerned about enrolling
them in our hearts, which requires a different type of
commitment.

The irrefutable understanding and practice associated
with Universal Truth II is that kids need Aces to succeed.
Some children get Aces, some don't. Adults control the Aces.
If kids are receiving Aces, it is because adults are giving them
and if they aren't, it is because adults are withholding them.
It is as simple as that.

Before we conclude this chapter, it is imperative that
we dispel a common myth that suggests that some people
are able to pull themselves up by their own bootstraps. That
is impossible. Everyone needs someone. It's a fact, and we
shouldn't minimize it by believing otherwise.

Chapter Six

Stories of Aces

Over the years, people have shared thousands of stories about how the Aces have been played in their lives. The Aces metaphor allows precise description. (Expressions like *good parents, good teachers, good role models,* and *good mentor* do not offer the depth of understanding about what children need from adults.) Being a parent, teacher, or mentor does not automatically shuffle up Aces. It is about how adults relate to children. Children and youth need different types of relationships at different times. Some adults can offer more than one Ace and others may be able to give a only a single Ace. Some adults can't reach some children, but all children can be reached by an adult. For example, a teacher may be able to give Aces to 90% of her/his students, but someone else needs to offer Aces to the other 10%.

Ace of Hearts
Never Too Late

Parent workshops help families understand that the cultural framework includes the home. To truly create a culture and not just another program, it is imperative that families see the value of adopting this framework. In doing so the shared belief statement then follows the child wherever he or she goes. The culture of Hope involves the entire community—families and all organizations.

In one of my workshops, "Successful Parents-Successful Children," we spend a fair amount of time reflecting on what parents offer that no other human can. The obvious answer is unconditional love. Of course, we explore that concept a little deeper so it doesn't become a cliché. Unconditional love including the caring for the child's physical and emotional well being, 24/7/365 is discussed, and how remarkable and powerful that role is!

One parent event was sponsored by an alternative high school. All the students who attended this school had struggled in their traditional high schools and most also had great difficulty at home. These youth had become disconnected—they lacked Aces. Fortunately, the personnel of the school where they were now enrolled understood their problems. They recognized that many of the behavioral issues affecting learning were also disturbing their emotional and social development. The school also empathized with the parents and their frustrations. Some of the parents felt helpless dealing with their children's challenges, which further fueled their frustrations and those of their children.

As the workshop focused on the unique and powerful role of the Ace of Hearts parents were refreshed with energy, hope, and stamina. They appreciated hearing about how truly irreplaceable they are in their child's life. They valued being reminded that their relationship difficulties were not insurmountable but required the opportunity to re-establish their role in their children's lives.

At the end of our evening workshop parents unanimously expressed gratitude:

"Thank you for reminding me how important I am in my child's life. In our day-to-day battles that understanding was lost."

"Thank you for reminding me it's never too late to make a difference in my child's life."

Ace of Clubs
Changing the Course of History

I've spent a fair amount of time in Springfield, Illinois, offering professional development classes. Most of the participants are teachers and youth workers. We speak about the Three Universal Truths and discuss the Aces— how some children get them and others don't.

During one visit, I stopped by a school I had trained the year before. A teacher approached me and shared the story of a sixth grader. Destiny was one of the worst behaved children in school. Her record supported that claim; detentions, suspensions, and a host of disciplinary challenges consumed Destiny's student file.

The day the teacher returned from attending our training, Destiny was having one of the worst of her many bad days. The teacher spoke to Destiny, and with these magic words changed the course of history: "Destiny," she said in her calmest voice, "you need to know something. You need to know that I love you."

Hearing those words, Destiny sobbed uncontrollably for five long minutes. The teacher helped the 11-year-old regain her composure. Even the teacher was surprised at Destiny's emotional reaction. What the teacher later learned was that Destiny had never been told "I LOVE YOU."

This is startling! What difference does anything make if you don't feel loved at any age, especially when you are 11? It really doesn't matter what disciplinary protocols or program a school has adopted. There are some things only a caring adult can achieve. In this case, the simple human expression of love was enough to have the teacher report that Destiny is now one of the best behaved students in school.

Ace of Spades
Saving a Future

You never know when you can save a future simply by dealing the Ace of Spades. A school counselor shared the following story.

During a visit to the school counselor, Josh blurted out, "That's not true." The startled counselor responded, "What's not true?"

"That poster," Josh said, pointing behind the counselor. The counselor turned around to see what the student was pointing at and noticed a poster that read, "All children are capable of success, NO Exceptions!"

"What do you mean that's not true?" quizzed the counselor. Without a moment's hesitation Josh barked back, "Well, my brother and I are not capable of success."

"Why do you say that?" she gently asked. With eyes now looking at the floor and in a much more subdued voice he struggled to get these words out, "Because my dad says we will amount to no good."

"Now, that's not true," offered the counselor.

"Yes, it is, and that's why I am in your office," replied Josh.

This being their first encounter, the counselor realized that she needed to know more about Josh. She needed to understand his academic and behavioral challenges. She wanted to know whether he was getting any Aces at school. He certainly was not getting them at home.

The counselor did call Josh's home. The boy's dad was raising him and his younger brother. Mom had passed away several years before. Most of the conversation between the counselor and the boy's father centered on the father's feelings that the boys were trouble to him and trouble to the school.

After the conversation with Josh's dad, the counselor visited Josh's teacher, who was at her wit's end as to what to do with him. She had 29 other students who also needed her attention. The counselor offered her help, and she began to tutor Josh. She helped him with a major school project on which he ultimately received a "B" grade; the highest score he had ever received.

He came by the counselor's office to share the good news. The first words out of his mouth were, "It is true; I am capable of success!" He then added, "We now have to help my brother."

It's amazing what can be achieved when caring adults believe in young people even when they don't believe in themselves.

Ace of Diamonds

Winning kids

The Ace of Diamonds is successfully dealt when children feel that they have succeeded. Most often our definition of success has to do with the expectations of adults or organizations. It's important to also consider the student's definition of success. Adults also need to be vigilant that when creating opportunities for some children to succeed they don't inadvertently create situations where others fail. In this case, we are most concerned with children where a pattern of failing is being established. There is absolutely no upside to failing a child. If success breeds success, then failure breeds failure.

Beyond grades, scores, and awards just a caring relationship can be the beginning of experiencing success. The following story illustrates that point.

Kevin is Going to Be in Trouble or He's Going to Be Successful—You Choose

Five-year-old Kevin, a kindergartener, was having the time of his life climbing up and sliding down the fireman's pole during recess. He was on the fireman's pole when the bell rang. Without thinking, Kevin slid down the pole and started walking to his class. So far, so good! No sooner had he taken 10 steps than he turned around and looked longingly at the fireman's pole. The classic battle between the school's rules and Mother Nature was played out on a school playground. Kevin couldn't help himself. How could he? Nature was not about to succumb to unnatural rules.

Of course Kevin ran back to the fireman's pole, climbed it as fast as he could and slid down it with great precision. All this happened under the watchful and trained eye of a para-educator responsible for supervising the kindergarteners during recess by ensuring that they return safely to their classroom when the bell rang. The extra time it took Kevin to run back to the pole and climb up and slide down now made him late. Rules are rules.

Kevin's realization began to sink in. Not only was he now late, the entire class had to wait until Kevin got in line. And to add insult to injury, Kevin had to pass the para-educator to get to his class.

One could only imagine what Kevin must have been thinking. He certainly had to expect the teacher's aide to stop him, waggle her finger and scold him for not only breaking a school rule but making his entire class wait.

The aide did indeed stop Kevin, but not to scold him. She took advantage of the moment to give Kevin the Ace of Diamonds.

"Kevin," she exclaimed, "you slid down the pole just like a real fireman. I bet you could be a firefighter some day. Now hurry, get to class."

With wide eyes, Kevin made a fist and a pumping gesture with his arm and yelled, "YES!"

Josh and Kevin's stories illustrate the power of giving Aces and highlight the type of culture that needs to exist for these opportunities.

Later on we will discuss the difference between culture and bureaucracy of our youth-serving organizations.

Chapter Seven

Universal Truth III
Mental Time Travel

The ability to remember the past and imagine the future are two capacities given little attention in the fields of education, child and youth development, even though these capacities can powerfully influence a child's life.

Scientists refer to the brain's ability to think about the past and future as *chronesthesia*, or mental time travel, hypothesized by Canadian psychologist Endel Tulving in the 1980s. Recently, much has been written about the brain's capacity to time travel. Most of it has to do with memory, as neuroscientists study why diseases such as dementia and Alzheimer's rob us of our past. Memory is a precious gift. If losing our memory robs us of our lives, then the inability to see our future has the same consequence.

In spite of adversity, some children do well while others struggle. This may be due to whether they learn to mentally time travel—past and future. The brain houses both capacities in the same area; therefore, without strong memory, future time travel is impossible.

Mental time travel also provides a strong clue about why children behave the way they do. Dr. James Garbarino has researched the causes of violent behavior by children and how they cope with stress. In an interview by *Perception* magazine in 2000 he was asked why adolescents appear to have an attitude that "It doesn't matter what happens to me." His answer addresses the theory of mental time travel:

> I think it speaks to two things. One is a lack of future orientation. Much of what we want kids to do, particularly teenagers, hinges on saying, "Do this as an investment for your future. . . . We know that some kids (and particularly kids who've experienced trauma) are likely to not have much future orientation; don't envision themselves in the future; and are more likely to have terminal thinking in which they barely exist in the present.

Children who have experienced trauma and make very poor decisions that highly impact their future do so because of two recurring themes that affect their ability to mentally time travel:

- First, their previous traumas result in a pattern of failure. This occurs because the brain's neuro pathways have established poor decision-making choices—their brains have been wired for poor choices. The option for making good choices, for whatever reasons, has not been established. The expression, "Success breeds success and failure breeds failure" supports this notion.

- Second, a brain's inability to draw on memories of success due to a pattern of bad choices limits its ability to successfully forecast its future. Terminal thinking occurs when the neuro pathways are not established, thereby blocking the brain's ability to mentally time travel.

Childhood educators must help wire the brain for good choices by teaching it how to mentally time travel—the default position is terminal thinking.

The work of Tulving and Gabarino lead us to a third universal truth. In formulating Universal Truth III, we concluded that children who achieve success possess the capacity to mentally time travel to their future: *Children succeed when they are able to articulate their future.*

When children/youth are able to see a future, create a roadmap to get there, and find the energy to direct their efforts, they dramatically increase their odds for success.

The ability to mentally time travel is a learned capacity. We teach children many skills and concepts they need in order to navigate through life: to tie their shoes, dress themselves, wipe their bottoms, write their names, read, drive a car. We teach them about character and societies, to understand math and science. Equal to all that, is the importance of teaching them about mental time travel.

The Psychology of Hope

The notion of future generates the concept of HOPE. We are grateful to the work of C. R. Snyder and Shane Lopez for their efforts and inspiration by illuminating our understanding of hope. Much of what we understand about hope is directly related to these great scholars.

Hope is the overall perception that one's goals can be met. According to Snyder (2000), hope has three necessary ingredients:

- Goal-oriented thoughts. Non-random human behaviors are directed by some goal, either short term or long term.

- Goals need to be of sufficient value to the individual so as to occupy conscious thought.

- Goals should be attainable yet challenging in nature - goals that are 100% likely to be achieved do not give people hope.

Pathways to Achievement
In order to achieve goals, people need to generate plausible routes. This type of thought process begins in infancy when cause-and-effect relationships are first being understood. Children see that certain actions influence events. Singular or multiple pathways need to be generated. In fact, alternative pathways should be generated when obstacles are faced. Those with the highest levels of hope tend to generate multiple pathways to goal achievement.

Agency Thoughts
In this motivational component to hope, people believe that they can initiate and sustain the pathways to goal achievement. This type of thought begins at one year of age when children realize they are actors who can influence their environment and initiate cause-and-effect relationships. The emphasis here is on thinking and not emotions, which are byproducts of hope. Positive emotions equal perceived success in achieving goals. Negative emotions equal perceived failure in achieving goals (Snyder, 2000).

Dr. Snyder died in January of 2006 at the age of 62. His colleague, Dr. Lopez, continues to discover links between hope, strengths development, academic success, and overall well-being. Dr. Lopez's commitment to studying hope and strengths enhancement for students from preschool through college graduation is helping to provide a roadmap for the psychological reform of American education. Dr. Lopez is now Senior Scientist in Residence at the Gallup Poll and father of the Gallup Student Poll in addition to serving as Research Director of the Clifton Strengths School.

The work of Snyder and Lopez has provided a more holistic understanding of the concept of hope and its relationship to mental time travel.

In 2008, I visited Dr. Lopez while he was associate professor at the University of Kansas and subsequently invited him to join the faculty of the 2009 Kids at Hope Youth Development Master's Institute held in cooperation with Arizona State University. Dr. Lopez's participation in our Institute was, and continues to be, helpful to advancing our work.

Similar to Snyder and Lopez we define hope as *the capacity to visit your future, return to the present, and prepare for the journey.*

We can witness this definition every day in the lives of children who play make believe. By watching little girls play house, for example, we observe *hope;* the girls are visiting their future, returning to the present, and preparing for the journey.

Defining Success

The word *success* seems to confound us. Ask 1,000 adults to define success and you will receive 1,000 different answers. In order to support a student's success we need a shared definition so that when we hear it or speak about it, we know what it means. That currently isn't the case. Most times when I introduce the expression "All children are capable of success," I am asked how I define success?

The word *success* is used so commonly that one would think we would have a common definition. We don't, but we need one to move forward in creating a culture where all children succeed.

Our work led us to three definitions. The first is a personal definition of success. Each individual has his or her own definition of what is success. Most equate success to achieving personal goals.

The second definition has to do with organizations. Everyone is affiliated by work or membership, formal or informal, with an organization. Each organization establishes its definition for success. Those definitions vary from organization to organization.

The third definition of success is cultural. It's the definition we share that creates a sense of community, "a greater common good." The cultural definition, however, does not replace either the personal or organizational definition. Once we agree on a cultural definition of success, we are able to work toward its achievement. The absence of a cultural definition prompts people to ask, "How do you define *success*?" At best, we have been limited to a personal definition or that of an organization. The absence of a shared definition sends differing messages to youth about our expectations. We need to be clear about our cultural definition.

The cultural definition came about by asking individuals to share personal examples of their success. We weren't interested in a generic or esoteric definition. We sought personal examples of success—specifics not generalizations. This query yielded a much more definitive understanding. Following are examples of the answers we received when we asked people to share personal and specific examples of success:

- I was the first in my family to graduate from high school.
- I was the first in my family to graduate from college.
- I have been happily married for 24 years.
- I have raised four wonderful children.
- I love my job.
- I ran my first marathon.
- I learned to fly fish.
- I won first place in a quilting contest.
- I learned to dance the tango.
- I started my own business.
- I love coaching a girl's softball team.
- I helped to build a home with Habitat for Humanity.
- I was chairman of my church's building campaign.
- I just bought my first home.
- I earned a master's degree.

Analysis of such examples revealed that people were saying that *success* was some*where*, not some*thing*. Certainly success was defined mostly in personal terms, which appeared to fall into four categories: home and family, education and career, community and service, and hobbies and recreation. Additionally, what we heard was that each definition was connected to a contribution. Success was somewhere (four destinations) and included a contribution at each destination. This idea that success was somewhere not something was an exciting finding, as it also helps to define *future*.

By pursuing this reasoning, we could then offer the following cultural definition of success: *Success is the result of knowing you have positively contributed to each of life's four destinations: home and family, education and career, community and service, and hobbies and recreation.*

Where is this Place We Call Future?

Within our cultural framework *future* is a holistic term. It doesn't exist in one dimension; it is multidimensional. When exploring the concept of future with children, we usually reduce it to one dimension, asking "What do you want to be when you grow up?" or "Where to you want to go to college when you graduate from high school?" Those two questions pretty much define the breadth of our efforts in exploring the concept of future. Yet, we know that *future* is more than a job, career, occupation, or continuing one's education. It shouldn't be reduced to two questions when there is so much more to explore.

Adults reported successes that occurred at four destinations, not just one. In other words, they discovered their future at four destinations. What, then, is the purpose of limiting a discussion about the future to just one or two dimensions when life is multidimensional? Instead, we need to ask, "Why do we teach what we teach in our schools and in our community based groups?" and "What is it that we are all working toward?"

Answers to those questions offer a clearer understanding and definition for the concept of *future*, which then connects directly to where adults identify their successes.

Therefore, all the knowledge, experiences, character, talent, and traits developed in youth are directed to four destinations:

• Home and family

• Education and career

• Community and service

• Hobbies and recreation

Our shared goal is to provide children the skill sets to navigate their lives to those four dominant destinations. This understanding is a far cry from "What do you want to be when you grow up?" These destinations become the basis for our definition of *future*: *Future lies at four destinations where we will journey and be expected to contribute.*

This is multidimensional and exciting. It gives meaning to learning math, reading, science, history, geography, music, art, physical fitness, sports, character, etiquette, and spirituality to name just a few of the many experiences we offer youth. Those subjects and experiences go beyond occupations. Each lesson contributes at each of life's four destinations. Reading is preparation for not only a job but to be a better parent, an informed voter, a contributing member of the community, and an opportunity to pursue a hobby. Math, science, history, and so on also become preparation for roles in all four of life's dominant destinations.

Defining and describing *future* as somewhere, which includes home and family, education and career, community and service, and hobbies and recreation, gives focus. By adopting that definition we are able to provide the guidance for children to set goals for their future. It also provides children the clarity needed to understand why they are studying, practicing and experiencing academics, sports, arts, character education, and other areas.

Each step in this process creates greater clarity in defining a culture where all children can succeed, no exceptions. We see the intersection between future and success as part of mental time travel thereby establishing its importance within Universal Truth III.

We are now meeting our fundamental definitions of culture offered by anthropology and psychology by describing why we do what we do for children. When the culture has a common definition for success, adults can support the journey from childhood to adulthood with greater focus and direction. We are far from that achievement today, but we are many steps closer than we were.

There is a downside to failure in effectively defining and practicing the type of culture required by youth. What results is a vacuum that may be filled by a subculture or series of subcultures. The following is an example of that danger.

A Subculture of Hopelessness

A few years ago, the television news magazine *60 Minutes* featured a segment about a 15-year-old who was a known gang member. She was asked about three small circle tattoos that appeared between her thumb and forefinger. She looked at her hand and explained that her tattoos represented her gang life and what she could expect from that existence. The first tattoo represented a hospital; the second, jail; and the third, a cemetery.

When a dominant culture fails to define itself, a vacuum is created. In this case, a gang subculture filled the void. It provided the answers that the dominant culture could not.

The need to know about our lives, why we are here and where we are going is universal. It's best when those answers come from a common set of values. That is the role of culture. In the case of the young gang member, the absence of that dominant culture resulted in a vaccum filled then by a subculture of hopelessness. Shortly after the interview, this beautiful young lady was killed by another gang member. Her tattoos were prophetic.

It is difficult not to think about what her life might have been if the Three Universal Truths had been in her culture and she had been able to mentally time travel to home and family, education and career, community and service, and hobbies and recreation instead of jail, hospital, and cemetery.

Chapter Eight

The Framework

From Bureaucracy to Culture and Back Again

We now have discussed the Three Universal Truths:

- Children succeed when surrounded by adults who believe they will succeed.

- Children succeed when they have meaningful and sustainable relationships with caring adults (four Aces).

- Children succeed when they can articulate their future (four destinations: home and family, education and career, community and service, and hobbies and recreation). That is called "mental time travel."

When the three Universal Truths are in place, a culture of hopefulness is created.

Our next challenge is to demonstrate the practical application of these truths. Just creating one program on top of other programs has not proven successful.

The Three Universal Truths require a cultural framework that supersedes, yet does not replace, all community programs. To house all programs created by various groups, we established the foundation with Universal Truth I. Then we put in place Universal Truth II as our first bearing wall. Universal Truth III forms the second bearing wall. The rooftop to our framework evidences the ultimate achievement of human potential: holistic success and self-actualization (see Figure 8.1).

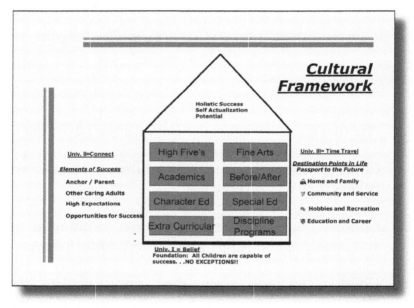

Figure 8.1 Cultural Framework

The strategic cultural framework is able to house all the separate and disconnected programs. The framework establishes a sense of community/culture. Every program, curriculum, or service offered to youth must connect to the Three Universal Truths in order to establish culture. The next challenge faced had to do with operationalizing the strategic cultural framework.

We know how to manage organizations, even small ones: We set up bureaucracies. Bureaucracy is a conglomerate that offers a system of operations. Max Weber, a German sociologist (1864-1920) outlined the key characteristics of a bureaucracy, many of which still define our organizations:

1. Specification of jobs with detailed rights, obligations, responsibilities, scope of authority system of supervision and subordination

2. Unity of command

3. Extensive use of written documents

4. Training in job requirements and skills

5. Application of consistent and complete rules (company manual)

6. Assign work and hire personnel based on competence and experience

By design, then, bureaucracies are created primarily for efficiency, not for innovation or effectiveness. What became clear was how the interrelationship between bureaucracy and culture determines the fate of organizations. What was additionally clear was that both bureaucracy and culture exist. We recognize these two systems as equal and dynamic forces ultimately determining the overall success of an organization. Bureaucracies focus on efficiency while culture focuses on effectiveness.

Figure 8.2 distinguishes the difference between these two dynamic opposing forces, bureaucracy and culture. Almost exclusively, organizations rely on the bureaucratic design to navigate their purposes. Though similar to Weber's description, our view of a bureaucracy incorporates the following characteristics and expanded definitions in order to compare those functions with those of a culture.

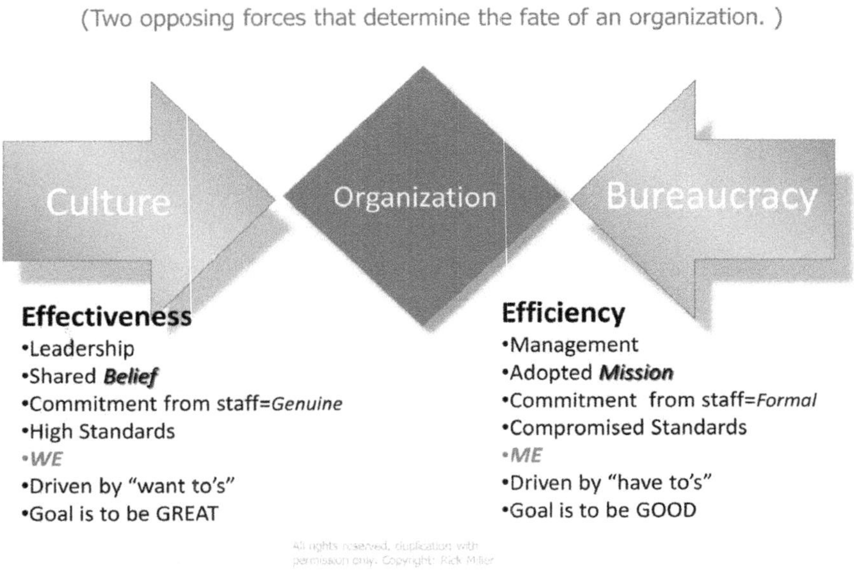
(Two opposing forces that determine the fate of an organization.)
Culture
Organization
Bureaucracy
Effectiveness
•Leadership
•Shared Belief
•Commitment from staff=Genuine
•High Standards
•WE
•Driven by "want to's"
•Goal is to be GREAT
Efficiency
•Management
•Adopted Mission
•Commitment from staff=Formal
•Compromised Standards
•ME
•Driven by "have to's"
•Goal is to be GOOD
All rights reserved, duplication with permission only. Copyright: Rick Miller

Figure 8.2. Culture vs. Bureaucracy/Systems

Bureaucracy

Management. Management is where the hierarchy exists. Who reports to whom for what functions? Job titles and descriptions are created from top to bottom.

Adopted mission. This is the organization's purpose for existence. It was written by a group of people with the expectation that anyone who works for the organization will commit to fulfill it.

Commitment of staff. This is formal. The expectation is an honest day's pay for an honest day's work. This commitment relies on the individual's need to work in order to meet his/her personal financial needs.

Personal efficacy. Personal efficacy means personal beliefs that define the strength of the individual's sense of personal mastery, one's confidence in her/his abilities to achieve goals.

Standards of performance/goal to be good. This is usually compromised because high performers and low performers cancel each other out, affecting an organization's potential.

Driven by have to. To ensure the operational side of the organization, there are non-negotiable functions (mandates) that must be performed.

Me. Every person has a defined role; the resulting dynamic is on the individual, or the ME (my job, my work, my performance review, my pay, who I report to, who reports to me).

Efficiency. Strict adherence to a hierarchy, separate job functions, and direct mandates results in efficiency but not necessarily effectiveness.

Culture

The other dynamic force, which has equal power in defining an organization, is culture. This particular force is ill defined in most organizations. Its power is, nonetheless, pronounced. An organization that cannot define and operationalize its culture creates a vacuum, which will be filled—usually by subcultures. Most subcultures ultimately work at cross-purposes with the mission of the organization.

The following characteristics define the culture of an organization.

Leadership. Cultures create an environment that encourages leaders to define themselves and offers the opportunity to maximize their talents.

Shared belief. Rather than a mission written by someone or some group for others, cultures rely on the shared beliefs of the individuals. These beliefs define the individual and when shared by the groupcreates culture. Mission statements only define the organization but not its people.

Genuine commitment of staff. Allegiance to the organization is the result of the individual's personal commitment to shared beliefs and mission of the organization. This is where the individual wants to work, not only to meet their financial needs but their emotional needs as well.

Collective efficacy. Collective efficacy is a group's confident expectation that it will successfully achieve its intended goal.

High standards/goal is to be great. Because the commitment is genuine and the beliefs between individuals are shared, the goal to be great not only represents the organization it equally represents how the individual values himself.

Driven by want to. This characteristic is expressed through a sense of ownership for the success of the organization.

WE. Cultures are by design not hierarchical. Cultures create interdependency and a sincere sense of the group.

To better understand how culture and bureaucracy are equally critical to the success of an organization we use a metaphor of a sailboat in open water (see Figure 8.3).

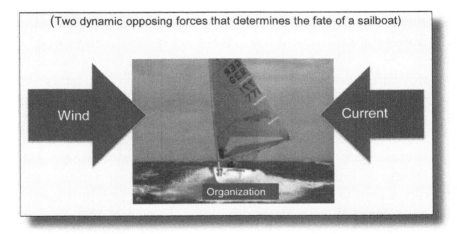

Figure 8.3. Wind and Current

The sailboat represents the organization. Wind represents bureaucracy, and current represents culture. To effectively navigate the sailboat the captain and crew must consider the power of both forces. If only bureaucracy (wind) is used, then culture (current) will affect the sailboat's ability to sail to its destination. If an organization overcorrects by only focusing on culture (current), then bureaucracy (wind) will force it off course. An effective captain and crew must learn to harness the power of both.

Bureaucracy is all about efficiency, and culture is where effectiveness exists. Yet, when organizations struggle to increase effectiveness, it usually looks to its bureaucracy. The answer lies in the culture.

The bureaucratic response to improving effectiveness is offered in new mandates through policies, reorganization, and budget adjustments. Most of these efforts are futile because effectiveness can be achieved only by the culture. Yet very little if any time is spent trying to harness this great force. That seems to occur because it's much easier to manage a bureaucracy than it is to lead a culture. To illustrate how a bureaucracy operates we share the following story.

As we have learned, bureaucracies are about efficiency not effectiveness. Each day, hundreds of thousands of school buses are dispatched to transport students from their neighborhoods to their schools. Buses pick up millions of students, drive them safely to their schools where aides greet them, check them in, accept excused absence notes, and ensure they are safely in their classrooms to begin the school day. Lessons are taught. Recesses, class breaks, and lunch are offered all on a strict schedule. Home and schoolwork are turned in, tests are administered, and information shared. After six or seven hours of these activities, millions of children are ushered back out to their designated school bus and returned safely home.

The process is repeated each day for approximately 180 days a year. The logistics are quite impressive. By and large, this part of our educational system works fairly well, because bureaucracies are designed for efficiency. However, the other part of education system is to educate children. That part needs quite a bit of improvement.

We can get millions of children to school, keep them pretty much engaged and return them home in the afternoon. In between, we struggle to educate them. The bureaucracy cannot help in that regard, although we futilely expect it to. It will never occur through bureaucracy. It will be achieved only when we learn to harness the power of the culture.

The culture is where the genuineness and passion for children is nurtured. It is where the "want to" lives, where the capacity to help "all children succeed, No Exceptions" thrives and where personal and shared responsibility, flourishes. It is where effectiveness is found.

We close this chapter with a poignant story that demonstrates why bureaucracies by themselves cannot be effective.

A Child Gifted HOPE

Patrick was 10 years old. He and his parents were from Nicaragua and living in the U.S. illegally. Patrick hadn't been feeling well for a while. He had severe headaches. His mother took him to a neighborhood doctor who referred Patrick to a pediatric neurologist at a well-known children's hospital. A social worker was assigned to assist the family with the arrangements. The parents confided in the social worker that they were in the country without legal papers and were concerned that they would be found out if required to fill out the paperwork needed for Patrick to see the specialist.

The social worker broke protocol, which is a kind way of saying she did what was right for the child, not for the bureaucracy. She took care of all the arrangements and told the parents everything would be fine and assuring them that no one would know of their situation. Patrick, his mother and father, and the social worker went to the hospital.

The neighborhood doctor's worse fears were realized: Patrick had a malignant and inoperable brain tumor. Upon learning of the test results, the social worker and the neurologist asked Patrick to wait with a hospital chaperone while they went to a conference room to break the news to the parents. Patrick asked if he could join them rather than remain in the waiting room, "If you are going to talk about me, I would like to be there." He joined his parents, the social worker, and the neurologist.

As the doctor spoke, the social worker interpreted for the parents. Patrick was bilingual; he heard the awful news before it was translated for his parents. He was given less than six months to live. The parents were inconsolable. Patrick understood the prognosis, and he asked to speak to the social worker alone. She obliged.

In confidence he asked for, as he said, "a big favor." Would she promise to contact the president of the United States? The social worker was taken aback by the request. She asked Patrick, "Why do you want me to contact the President of the United States?"

"Because," he said, "I need him to help my parents when I die."

"How can he do that?" she asked, her voice breaking a little.

"I would ask him if he could help make my parents legal so they wouldn't have to worry anymore. I would ask him to help my parents get a house. And I would ask him if he could make sure that I would be buried next to my grandfather in Nicaragua."

The social workers eyes filled with tears. Without thinking, she said, "Sure!"

Patrick hugged her and went back to his parents.

She told her supervisor what had happened. The supervisor reprimanded her, saying, "How could you make such a promise? Not only did you break policy, but you made a promise you cannot possibly keep."

The social worker responded by saying she did not promise Patrick that the president would grant his three wishes but only that she would contact him. "I could at least do that for the boy," offered the social worker. The supervisor left quite angrily. The social worker kept her promise.

A couple months after the letter was sent, the White House called her. Unfortunately, they said the president would be out of the country for a period of time, but the first lady would very much like to meet and talk with Patrick. The social worker could not believe her ears. How could this happen? But it did. Arrangements were made for Patrick to meet the first lady of the United States. While schedules were being cleared, Patrick was admitted to the hospital as the tumor was taking its toll. The first lady agreed to meet Patrick in the hospital.

A week before the scheduled visit, Patrick called the social worker. "Hi," he said when he heard her voice. "Hi to you," was her response. She was so happy to hear from Patrick. "What's up?" she asked. "You getting excited to see the first lady?"

Patrick did not answer the question. Instead he said, "I just wanted to call you and say thank you and good bye."

A few hours later that day, Patrick died.

Hope is a powerful force in life and death. The first lady helped Patrick's parents obtain legal residence status and find a suitable home. Patrick was laid to rest next to his grandfather.

Chapter Nine

The Strategic Framework in Action

In the previous chapters we have explored, reviewed, and discussed the Three Universal Truths found throughout the literature where the focus is child and youth development. In this chapter we demonstrate the unique, powerful, and simple adaptation of these truths.

During our workshops and classes we invite one adult participant to join us at the front of the class. This volunteer represents an eighth grade female student. We then ask another participant to come forward to represent a caring adult. This could be a teacher or administrator. The following is the scenario we outline for the class.

The eighth grade student is a recent transfer. The caring adult is reviewing her file, which includes the following data:

- The student is 13 years old.

- She has attended three middle schools in the past year and a half.

- She is on probation for shoplifting.

- She lives in a foster home.

- She has lived in four foster homes since she was eight years old.

- She was expelled two years ago for smoking on campus and starting a fight.

- She is currently reading at the fourth grade level and also struggles with math.

- She takes medication for Attention Deficit Hyperactive Disorder.

- She has poor interpersonal skills and is found very much to be a loner.

After reviewing that litany of issues we note to the class and the volunteer representing the caring adult that "This is what the student brings to you. What do you bring to the student that can dramatically transform her from at risk to at hope?"

We then introduce and demonstrate what Ann Masten, University of Minnesota and a member of our 2010 Youth Development Master's Institute faculty, calls "ordinary magic."

Resilience is common and it typically arises from the operation of normal rather than extraordinary human capabilities, relationships, and resources. In other words, resilience emerges from ordinary magic (Masten, 2010).

Our expression of how ordinary magic looks is described by the following:

We ask our caring adult to frame with his hands and fingers the face of the "eighth grade student" similar to that of a movie director visualizing a scene. (See picture below.)

By this expression we are creating a mental blueprint where we can use the Three Universal Truths to respond to the statement and question, "We now know what the student brings to you. What will you bring to the student that can dramatically transform her from risk to hope?"

The two thumbs represent Universal Truth I: believing that all children can succeed, no exceptions! This is the foundation to our strategic cultural strategy and framework.

The left hand represents Universal Truth II: meaningful and sustainable relationships represented by the four fingers of the left hand—Ace of Hearts (anchor parent); Ace of Clubs (other caring adults); Ace of Spades (high expectations); Ace of Diamonds (opportunities to succeed). This hand represents our first bearing wall.

The right hand represents Universal Truth III: articulating the future (mental time travel). The destinations are represented by the four fingers of the right hand—home and family, education and career, community and service, and hobbies and recreation. This hand becomes the second bearing wall.

We now have a framework using the Three Universal Truths represented by our hands and fingers. We are ready to respond to the critical statement and question—what the student brings and how the adult responds.

The caring adult's response:

Welcome to our school. It looks like you have had your fair share of challenges. Those are important for us to know. More importantly, is how we can go forward together. Let me share with you how that will happen.

First, at our school, we believe all our students are capable of success and there are no exceptions. We believe you will be successful here.

Second, at our school, we want you to know that we ensure that each student has a meaningful and sustainable relationship with a caring adult, hopefully with more than one. We want you to feel connected and supported.

Third, we will work with you so that you can visualize and talk about an exciting future where you will succeed at four destinations: home and family, education and career, community and service, and hobbies and recreation.

When a school's culture is effectively defined by the Three Universal Truths, those words become genuine. The understood goal then is students bring the past—adults offer a future.

Chapter Ten

Are You a Treasure Hunter?

Think about your own job history. How many different titles have you held during your teen and adult years? Consider, too, the purpose of each of the titles. Titles are all about the bureaucracy. They are focused on the efficiency of the organization. From chief executives, superintendents, directors, assistants, principals, supervisors, managers, teachers, coordinators, workers, aides, and so forth—the goal is to get the work done.

When we sponsor classes, workshops, institutes or seminars, we usually ask the participants to raise their hands if they hear their official bureaucratic title announced. Typically it looks and sounds like this:

How many superintendents or directors are represented? Usually a hand or two are raised.

How many assistant superintendents/directors are present? An additional two or three hands go up.

If you are a principal or assistant principal or a branch manager, raise your hand. Three to four hands are sighted.

Teachers, instructional coaches, program directors, and coordinators or counselors are asked to identify themselves, and they do.

We suggest that what was just offered was the opportunity to witness bureaucracy. To operate each organization requires various positions. Each has a job title and a job description given by the bureaucracy.

It's now time to describe culture. We follow the same format, but this time we ask all participants to raise their hands if they are Treasure Hunters. The resulting action is quite dramatic: All the hands in the room are raised.

Bureaucracies require a hierarchy to support efficiency. *Cultures* necessitate shared titles to support effectiveness.

Even within our participating schools and youth organizations, children, youth, parents, and the general public understand how the bureaucracy operates. They know what a principal does. They know who generally reports to whom and who is in charge of what.

But does the same understanding exist when asked about the culture of the organization? The answer is no. We have done a good job explaining our organizations bureaucratically, but have not done as well when defining them culturally.

When asked to share examples of their daily tasks, participants report stark differences among their functions associated with their titles.

Within the strategic cultural framework we acknowledge the importance of bureaucracy and the necessity of different titles and separate job functions. But it is equally important that we define how the treasure hunter's title is critical to defining culture.

Regardless of your bureaucratic title in an organization, you can also have a cultural title. We offer the title of *Treasure Hunter*. Furthermore, we demonstrate the importance of all treasure hunters sharing the same responsibilities:

- All treasure hunters believe all children are capable of success, no exceptions!

- All treasure hunters ensure that children have meaningful and sustainable relationships with caring adults.

- All treasure hunters are committed to teaching children the power of time travel (articulating their futures at four destinations: home and family, education and career, community and service, and hobbies and recreation.

Over the years many of our "graduates" have acknowledged this understanding by adding to the business cards their cultural title alongside their bureaucratic one. Here are some examples:

City of Glendale

GLENDALE

Brent Ackzen
Bureau Commander
"Treasure Hunter"
Glendale Police Department

6835 N. 57th Drive • Glendale, Arizona 85301
623-930-3251 • (Fax) 623-931-2103
Email: brent@ci.glendale.az.us
"Community and Police working in partnership"

CARTWRIGHT SCHOOL DISTRICT #83

Kay Coleman
Assistant Superintendent of Educational Services
Treasurer Hunter

3401 N. 67th Avenue   Fax: (623) 691-5922
Phoenix, AZ 85033   kcoleman@mail.cartwright.k12.az.us
(623) 691-4025

American Red Cross
We'll Be There

Tara Roberts

Treasure Hunter
Youth Program Specialist

 A United Way Agency

Central Arizona Chapter
6135 North Black Canyon Hwy.   Tel: (602) 336-6464
Phoenix, AZ 85015-1892   Fax: (602) 336-5781
http://www.redcross.org   E-mail: robertsta @usa.redcross.org

To reinforce the importance and power of understanding the shared responsibilities of a treasure hunter we encourage our partner organizations to share this pledge with their children:

Treasure Hunters Pledge

As an adult and a treasure hunter, I am committed to searching for all the talents, skills, and intelligence that exist in children. I believe that all children are capable of success, No Exceptions!

By adopting this practice, the entire organization—all staff and all children—understand the remarkable balance between bureaucracy and culture.

We've witnessed the pledge being recited by teachers at the beginning of each classroom day. We've also witnessed all the food service personnel, custodial, and maintenance staff doing the same thing.

We have heard stories from some schools that the students will not let the day start unless they hear the adults recite the treasure hunters' pledge.

At an all-girl alternative high school in St. Lucie County, Florida, the students—many of whom have dropped out of school, have children of their own, or are on probation—are having difficulty finding their way through life. They shared how important it is for them to hear their teachers and staff recite the pledge. For whatever reason, their traditional school had not been able to meet their challenging needs; the bureaucracy, regardless of how hard it tried, did not work for them. What did work was a culture of treasure hunters.

Chapter Eleven

Top Five Practice # 1

Believed and Practiced Here

Over next five years, after launching our cultural strategic framework, we watched, consulted, and supported organizations that shared our vision where all children succeeded, No Exceptions. We learned how the Three Universal Truths were to be practiced within the culture of an organization rather than by its bureaucracy. We were moving from theory and research on to practice.

What We Discovered

The first practice was to share and celebrate the belief. This is what we learned: There is a major difference between believing in something and practicing it. Many people know the value of good nutrition and exercise but fail to practice it. There is also a major difference between practicing something and believing in it. Many who work in schools and youth organizations do not believe that all children can succeed. A bureaucracy can exist without a shared cultural belief and, theoretically, a culture can exist without a defined bureaucracy; however, to achieve efficiency and effectiveness requires a balance of both.

The following is a simple illustration demonstrating the differences between believing and practicing and bureaucracy and culture.

The Friendly Place

A friend, who was the executive director of a large youth-serving organization, asked me to help the staff identify its core values.

This staff meeting was scheduled for 1 p.m. on a Tuesday afternoon. When I arrived at the agency at 12:45, two other people were waiting to introduce themselves to the receptionist. While waiting in line, I witnessed the activity of the staff. Two colleagues were visiting a few feet from the receptionist desk, another was on her way from one office to the other crossing through the receptionist area, and a third was looking for a file he had left with the receptionist sometime earlier. They all seemed pretty busy and certainly focused on their work.

A few minutes later I introduced myself and was warmly greeted by the nice receptionist. She recognized my name and directed me down a hallway to the first room on the right. She said the staff should be joining me shortly.

At 1 p.m. the staff arrived, and we all introduced ourselves. I then asked about the purpose of the meeting. It was confirmed that we were to identify the core values of their organization.

As the group's facilitator, I asked them what they would like the public to say about them. How would they like to be known? One person speaking for the group said that they wanted their organization to be known as "friendly."

"Good," I replied and wrote the word *friendly* on the whiteboard. I then asked what the word meant. The group seemed perplexed by my question. I assume they were thinking, "Why is he asking that? Everyone knows what friendly means." *Friendly* is not a word people normally run to the dictionary to look up.

I explained that I was asking the question because of a recent experience: I had been asked to join them at 1 p.m.; when I arrived at 12:45 p.m., two people were lined up to introduce themselves to the receptionist. I got in line to wait my turn.

While waiting, I noted that three of them either had walked by me, were in the same area I was, or had seen me waiting. Not one took the initiative to welcome me to their agency and ask if they could offer some help considering the receptionist seemed busy.

In other words what does *friendly* look, sound, or feel like at their agency? Did they feel that it was only the job of the receptionist to greet visitors? It would have taken, at most, only 30 seconds to come up to me as I was waiting in line and say something like, "Hi, my name is_____. It appears our receptionist is busy. May I help you?"

My reaction would have been, "Wow, what a friendly and helpful organization." Instead it was obvious that their bureaucracy was well defined with strict job descriptions and functions, but they needed to better understand their culture where the belief and practice of "friendly" actually exists.

Big Vision Needs a Culture

A few years ago, I had the opportunity to meet with the superintendent of one of our country's largest school systems. The day before we were to meet the superintendent delivered his State of the District message. There was one statement in it he repeated for emphasis: "If you only remember one thing today, remember that 'all our students will be college bound.'"

When we met the next day, I asked him about that statement. He was, of course, proud of it. What I wanted to know was how the powerful statement would be translated into action. What will the bus drivers, cafeteria people, custodians, teachers, para-educators, and counselors do differently to realize such a goal. That powerful of a vision cannot be mandated or directed to just a segment of the education system or community. "All children, college bound," requires a cultural shift not a new program; one that is believed and practiced by all.

By and large, organizations do a great job defining their missions, visions, core values, goals, and objectives. But attempting to translate those statements culturally is where the difficulties are found.

According to Anthony Mohammad, who writes extensively about school culture, he identifies four types of personalities that make up our educational institutions. I would add that these traits exist in many of our other youth-serving bureaucracies as well. He describes the fundamentalists, tweeners, survivors, and believers. The fundamentalists are the veterans of the system. These self-proclaimed realists know what's going to happen before it happens. They crave the power and work diligently to control the process for fear if they don't, something could change and threaten them. The tweeners are either new to the profession or to the organization and its culture, usually in it for one to three years. They are vulnerable to being co-opted by either the fundamentalists or the believers. The survivors have weathered all the storms associated with bureaucracy and are for the most part burned out but still stay around. The believers entered the youth service/education business believing they could help children succeed, and their commitment and enthusiasm for that achievement hasn't changed.

In their behavior, fundamentalists are quite vocal and politically savvy. They know who the believers are and they leave them alone as they do the survivors. They set their eyes on the tweeners who have yet to find their place. Unfortunately, believers go about their business very privately. They aren't seeking recruits. They don't want to get caught up in the politics of a bureaucracy and are happy to be left alone to make the difference they know they are making with their students.

Somewhat similar to Dr. Mohammad's observations, I have come to identify four types of employees, two of which fall within the bureaucratic dimension and two within the culture.

Lip Service Employees

The first is lip service employees. They easily slip in to a bureaucratic focused organization primarily because they meet the general qualifications. Most bureaucracies hire using the following criteria: experience and credentials. Lip service employees know that and use it to their benefit; they say what the need to say to get a job. These people are found out quickly and referred to as bad hires. The unfortunate side is they can do much harm in a short time.

Formal Employees

Formal employees also are found in bureaucracies. Their motto is "an honest day's work for an honest day's pay." Their hearts aren't in their work and they do the minimum to maintain their employment status. They need a job and one job is as good as another.

Genuine Employees

Next we identify the genuine employee. This person has made a personal commitment to a field of work. It's more than a job. He brings more than his body to work by offering a level of energy needed for achievement. He offers a sense of pride in his accomplishments and feels a sense of camaraderie with his colleagues.

Leader Employees

The fourth category is the leader employee. This person, by personal and professional commitment, best represents that which the organization stands for. The organization's mission and shared beliefs are manifested in this person's work. He or she may or may not be a leader as defined by the bureaucracy but is nonetheless acknowledged for remarkable leadership.

By exploring the personality traits and characteristics of the people whose job it is to support children's development we can better understand why some organizations are effective and others aren't.

We now can distinguish between *ME* and *WE*. *ME* is found on the bureaucratic side; this is where the *lip service* and *formal employees* exist. *Believers* are also part of the *ME* class. At first glance it would appear a school or youth group would want the believers working for them. But our concern is that if they remain in the *ME* category, focused only on the children in their charge and not the entire organization, they would limit the opportunity to create a culture where all children succeed.

For example, as a *believer*, I (*ME*) can help some children succeed, but *WE* can help all children succeed. In order to support the success of all children, not only those assigned to us, we must look to culture for guidance. It comes in the form of *WE*.

*WE*s are the *genuine* and *leader* employees.

The Starfish Story

Most people in the youth-serving business are familiar with the starfish story. Our version, however, has a different ending.

As the story goes, a hiker comes to a bluff overlooking the ocean. He notices a man walking up and down the seacoast picking up starfish that have been washed ashore. He picks up a starfish and tosses it back into the ocean and then picks up another and tosses it back as well. The hiker becomes mesmerized by this exercise, primarily because there were literally thousands of starfish washed ashore. He can't resist descending the bluff to speak to the man tossing back the starfish.

"I've been watching you for the better part of an hour," the hiker confesses, "and I am amazed at what you are doing. It seems so futile; you are picking up one starfish at a time returning it to the ocean, and yet there are so many starfish still left on shore. How do you hope to make a difference?"

After listening to the question, the Good Samaritan reached down to the sand, picked up another starfish, and tossed it back into the water. Then he looked at his inquisitor and said, "Just made a difference for that one."

Many people who hear that story are moved by its simplicity of effort and cause. It seems to remind all of us that one person can make a difference regardless of how small and in spite of the great odds.

Although, I too, am moved by the starfish story and its moral, I cannot help but think about all the other starfish left on the shore. Without minimizing the impact and importance of the starfish story, we do need to pause and recognize we must not be content with helping one child at a time. We cannot leave others behind and we cannot do this work alone.

It reminds us of our goal, mission, and vision to support the success of all children. This cannot succeed without unleashing the power of a culture and that can be achieved only by effectively using the *WE* in our strategic cultural framework.

The obvious conclusion from this discussion is the importance of celebrating our belief that all children are capable of success, no exceptions! The culture should amplify that statement. Everyone and anyone in the organization and ultimately within the community should offer it. An organization—the crossing guard, custodian, directors, teachers, program staff, food service, everyone—who believes and practices the belief that all children can succeed, no exceptions, should receive any visitor accordingly.

*"Welcome to our school/organization/community, where **we all believe** all children are capable of success, No Exceptions!"*

Can you hear how that sounds? Can you imagine the power inherent in that phrase? Everyone says, hears, rejoices, and practices it.

Chapter Twelve

Top Five Practice #2

The Pledge: Power of Self-Talk

The prestigious Mayo Clinic published the following article about self-talk.

Positive thinking often starts with self-talk. Self-talk is the endless stream of unspoken thoughts that run through your head every day. These automatic thoughts can be positive or negative. Some of your self-talk comes from logic and reason. Other self-talk may arise from misconceptions that you create because of lack of information.

If the thoughts that run through your head are mostly negative, your outlook on life is more likely pessimistic. If your thoughts are mostly positive, you're likely an optimist—someone who practices positive thinking.

Researchers continue to explore the effects of positive thinking and optimism on health. Health benefits that positive thinking may provide include

- increased life span,
- lower rates of depression,
- lower levels of distress,
- greater resistance to the common cold,
- better psychological and physical well-being,
- reduced risk of death from cardiovascular disease, and
- better coping skills during hardships and times of stress (Mayo Clinic, 2011).

An expert in human development, Martin Seligman, former president of the American Psychological Association and founder of the Positive Psychology movement, stated in 1990 that, "Our thoughts are not merely reactions to events; they change what ensues." (*Learned Optimism*, 1990)

Schools and other child development organizations understand that power. We learned from them that practicing the belief that all children are at hope requires that we share that belief with students. Since the mid-1990s, Kids at Hope, in alignment with its Three Universal Truths, has promoted the practice of positive self-talk by encouraging recitation of the following pledge:

I am a Kid at Hope
I am talented, smart, and capable of success
I have dreams for the future, and I will climb to reach those goals and dreams every day

It's unimaginable that anything could be simpler than learning and practicing this personal affirmation every day. It sets the affective grounding for all other learning to take root.

Hundreds of schools and youth-serving groups across the United States share the power of this pledge. At the time of publication, we estimate that well over 400,000 students recite and practice the pledge daily. It may be the second most recited pledge in the U.S. after the Pledge of Allegiance, but with over 50 million students in grades k-12, we are a long way from maximizing its power.

Sarah's Story

Sarah was in eighth grade when her middle school introduced the Kids at Hope pledge. Leadership lacked excitement or interest in asking 13- and 14-year-olds to recite those words; the adults were certain that middle school students would fine the pledge lame, uncool, cheesy, and just plain boring. Teachers already had so much to do each day that there was not enough time to add anything else.

We persisted with the teachers and administration: The research is clear—students who learn and practice positive affirmations do better in life than students who don't. Ultimately the school acquiesced and introduced the pledge. During the first few weeks, the practice of the pledge came across awkward . . . okay, it was "cheesy."

By the end of the first month the recitation of the pledge was less lame. By the end of second month, the day started with the pledge as though it had always been part of the school's culture. We knew that it was important but we couldn't imagine how important it was to be for Sarah.

Sarah and her mother lived alone in Phoenix, Arizona. Sarah's father had abandoned the family years ago and they had no contact with him. Sarah's older brother was more than 1,500 miles away, in Washington, DC, soon to be deployed to Afghanistan.

Sarah's mom worked the midnight shift but made it home before Sarah woke up each morning to help ready her for school; it was their mother-daughter time. Mom made Sarah breakfast and helped her get off to school.

While Sarah was at school, Mom slept and was up by the time Sarah returned home. She loved to hear about Sarah's school adventures. They prepared dinner together and Mom offered what help she could with Sarah's homework. At almost 10 p.m., Sarah prepared for bed. Mom made sure Sarah was safely and soundly asleep then prepared to go to work. Long days!

One morning, Sarah awoke and her mom was not there to greet her. Instead a neighbor lady was there. "Sarah, your mom became sick at work last night, and they had to take to her to the hospital," came the terrifying news. Sarah quickly dressed and the neighbor drove her to the hospital. One can only imagine what thoughts were swirling in Sarah's mind. When she arrived at her mom's bedside, Sarah realized how grave the situation was. Her mother was on a respirator; she had suffered a brain aneurysm and was diagnosed as being brain dead.

The decision to take her off the respirator was made, and a priest was summoned to deliver the last rites. As the priest entered the room, Sarah walked to her mother's side, reached for her hand and said, "I am a kid at hope. I am talented, smart, and capable of success. I have dreams for the future, and I will climb to reach those goals and dreams every day."

I asked Sarah why she chose the Kids at Hope pledge to recite to her mother at that time.

"My school taught it to me and I wanted my mother to die peacefully," she shared. "I thought that if she knew I was *at hope*, she could pass knowing I was going to be okay."

With Sarah's permission I continue to share her story with as many people as I can as a reminder that HOPE is a gift that must be given. Sarah's middle school now understands that power.

Sometimes we need more hope than at other times. It's important we have it available for the times, big and small, whenever we need it.

Time and time again, teachers who have adopted the pledge report that whenever students complain that something is too hard or they can't do it or aren't smart enough, the teacher reminds them of their pledge. The students understand the concept and return to their work believing in their own efficacy.

The pledge is a powerful tool that we should use to support the development of children.

Chapter Thirteen

Top Five Practice # 3
The Report Card

To maximize an organization's capacity to perform efficiently and effectively, both bureaucracy and culture need to be harnessed. Yet, we continue to disproportionately focus on the bureaucracy and ignore the culture.

Practice number 3 helps to correct that imbalance. To achieve a balance, we recommend creating a report card that helps children see their many other assets and strengths beyond what is required to be assessed by the bureaucracy.

Once a year, each child should receive such a report card focused entirely on strengths and assets. These findings differ from what is normally recorded in a student's transcript or portfolio.

Much of the thinking behind the development of this type of report card is credited to Howard Gardner's theory of Multiple Intelligence. Gardner, an educational psychologist at Harvard University, suggests that people have various kinds of intelligences. He defines *intelligence* as "*the capacity to solve problems or to fashion products that are valued in one or more cultural settings*" (Gardner & Hatch, 1989).

Our interpretation of Gardner's work suggests there are many ways to be smart. We then define *smart* as *what the world needs and what you have.*

The obvious point is made when we ask, "Does the world need people with a sense of humor?" If you have that skill, trait, or characteristic, you are smart. Does the world need people with integrity? If you possess that, you are smart. Also included would be those intelligences measured by traditional grading systems, intelligence exams, and psychometrics.

Many educators and policy makers support Gardner's theory. According to Mindy L. Kornhaber (2001)

> ... the theory validates educators' everyday experience; students think and learn in many different ways. It also provides educators with a conceptual framework for organizing and reflecting on curriculum assessment and pedagogical practices. In turn, this reflection has led many educators to develop new approaches that might better meet the needs of the range of learners in their classrooms (p. 276).

Unfortunately, what we know about how children succeed still gets lost. Much of why we see a narrow definition of success translated by test scores is traced to the National Commission on Excellence in Education 1982 report entitled, "A Nation at Risk," which found that 14% of 17-year-olds were functionally illiterate, 40% of minority children were functionally illiterate, 70% of high school students could not solve multi-step mathematics problems, and 80% of high school students could not write a persuasive essay.

The Commission recommended that schools strengthen high school graduation standards, adopt measurable rigorous academic standards, increase learning time, and raise teacher qualifications.

That report ushered in new era in education. Child and youth development organizations had to pay attention to the report's findings if they were to be considered relevant. The nation has spoken. Not only did it institutionalize the expression *at risk*, it became the basis for the No Child Left Behind Legislation signed into law in 2002. A follow-up report published in 2003 entitled *Our Schools and Our Future: Are We Still at Risk?* found that educational results had not improved since the publication of the original report two decades earlier.

Elementary, middle, and high schools were now given performance standards for reading, mathematics, and science. High stakes testing was required to determine if standards were being met and there were penalties for not meeting those standards.

We know that other skills, talents, characteristics, and traits including HOPE do have value and that we must create opportunities to recognize and nurture them. Why then have we decided not to focus on the whole child and reduce a child's development to three intelligences?

One major reason is found in James C. Collins and Jerry I. Porras' book, *Built to Last* (1997). Their explanation describes "The Tyranny of the Or," the concept that "you cannot live with two seemingly contradictory ideas at the same time" (p. 43). In this argument, we see institutions choosing either academics or the whole child as their primary focus. Unfortunately, that is a false choice. The real answer is also revealed by Collins and Porras when they identify "The Genius of the And" (1997). In other words, both can and must happen at the same time.

Collins and Porras explain:

The Tyranny of the OR pushes people to believe that things must be either A OR B, but not both. Instead of being oppressed by the Tyranny of OR, highly visionary organizations liberate themselves with the Genius of the AND; the ability to embrace both extremes of a number of dimensions at the same time. Instead of choosing between A or B, they figure out a way to have both A AND B (pp. 43-44).

It's not incongruent, then, to be able to focus on academic skills including reading, math, and science along with the multiple intelligence theorized by Howard Gardner, the Gallup Poll's Student StrengthQuest, and offered as a practice by our work. In other words, there is a way to focus on the whole child by embracing the "The Genius of the And" while ignoring the "Tyranny of the OR."

In that spirit then, we can offer both an academic report card as well as the strengths-based report card, which is quite simple and remarkably powerful. The whole idea of this report card is to validate and document potential rather than just behavior.

Most formal reports about children are based on narrow assessments and cover areas that include academic, social, emotional, and physical elements. They apply a range of norms to determine whether a child is above average, average, or below average. We report on these matters without fully understanding their lifelong ramifications for the child.

Negatively labeling a child never helps. At best it stereotypes, which is mostly used to devalue people. Here is an excerpt from Charles Appelstein's book, *No Such Thing as a Bad Kid* (1998) that underscores this point:

Steering Clear of Labels

Responding sensitively also requires us to refrain from negative labeling. Why? Because when we attach a pejorative label to a child, it sticks. We, and everyone we have spoken to, begin to see the child for what he does rather than who he is.

Suppose you are deciding between two children who are on a waiting list for admission to your group. The first child has lived in four foster homes and has burn marks on his hands, which have been traced to abuse by his father; he is portrayed as a sad and lonely boy who has never had a friend and does not trust adults. The second youngster is described as self-absorbed, manipulative, incapable of following directions, in constant need of attention, and willing to do anything to get it. Which child would you choose? Most people who are asked this question select kid number one.

In actuality, these descriptions are from two profiles of the same child; only the wording is different. Describe a child's painful history and people want to reach out to him; label his annoying behaviors, and people are less willing to help (p. 19).

If required to assess children against some criteria, we should also include one additional standard of great importance. Let's add treasure-hunting skills and identify "potential"—*buried treasures that when discovered can help develop a sense of hopefulness and assist the student in defining, planning, and succeeding.*

We call this document a report card because our culture has elevated that term to high importance and stature. As children enter the formal world of child development and education, they repeatedly and regularly receive some formal assessment that identifies their strengths and weaknesses. We will forevermore document children as above average, average, or below average. Through this process, children and youth receive an image of very smart, smart, not so smart, or possibly even stupid. This special report card provides the balance to the strict academic report card. When used by a skilled and caring adult, this report card can truly be transformative because it can unleash a child's potential.

Below is a list of helpful hints to maximize the power of such a report card. It is to be used as an expression of hope and success for all children, without exception! Remember: It's about taking the time to identify strengths and assets in children—even the hidden ones.

- **Be sincere**. One cannot fake genuine behavior. Children know whether it is authentic or whether one just went through the motions to complete another required task.

- **Take your time even though this type of report card doesn't require much time.** By this we mean begin completing the report cards well before they are due; don't wait until the last minute. We have seen too many situations when caring adults and teachers wait until the last minute and struggle with the quality of treasure hunting needed to be authentic. Each report card requires only about five minutes. Doing one a day for 30 days is much easier than 30 in one night.

- **Connect to real-world value/destinations.** Once you have identified three to six treasures, assets, and/ or strengths in a child (not those that are reported scholastically, academically, or socially on the traditional report card, but those that might go undiscovered), connect the treasure(s)/asset(s) and/or strength(s) to real-world value related to life's four major destination points. For example, what is the value of a sense of humor, or sincere smile, or helpfulness to home and family, education and career, community and service, and hobbies and recreation?

- **Define smart.** Help students process that smart means *what the world needs and what you have,* and how this definition applies to them.

- **Talk about their strengths and how they relate to their future.** This creates rapport (Aces relationship). This report card is a 100% positive experience for both the student and the caring adult.

Other Hints

- Learn to change negative attributes to positive attributes so you can turn a negative into a positive (i.e., *whining* can be defined as *expressive. Argumentative* can be *debater; negative* can be *analytical, obstinate* can be *confident.* Use your imagination).

- Keep a list of expressions of words that represent treasures/assets/strengths.

- If you believe you are an Ace but students do not name you as a caring adult or as one of their Aces, tell them to put your name down or help them identify other Aces whom they may have forgotten. Children need to know they have adults who care about them. Do not keep this a secret.

- Note that completing the report card is also a challenge for students who are not sure what you are expecting. Be clear about this experience for your own sake and that of the student.

- Help any students who seem unable to identify their other talents. That is the same with all the questions in the report card. The important concept to remember is at the end of this experience you have helped to discover treasures and translated those treasures into *hope* and a plan to achieve success at one or more of life's destination points. What can be more powerful or valuable than that experience?

To demonstrate the effectiveness of this type of report card, we offer the following case study as part of our in-service training. The instructions offered during the in-service are that

- participants are to identify all the strengths, positive characteristics, traits, and talents offered within the case study; and

- after hearing the study, participants have only 20 seconds to complete their inventory.

Case Study
Timmy, age 10

Timmy is in fifth grade. He struggles academically and sometimes behaviorally. Timmy typically received Cs and Ds on his assignments, tests, and report card. He received an F in one course. He did make a B on a spelling test. He is frequently scolded for daydreaming and being off-task. Usually at these times he is drawing elaborate designs and airplanes.

Timmy has to walk his kindergarten-age sister to her class every day. He hates doing it and complains constantly about it. Similarly, he is required to pick her up from her class at the end of the day and walk her home before he is permitted to play or hang out with his friends.

Timmy loves sports, but his temper usually gets the best of him. When he feels a call by an umpire or referee is not just, he argues with the official.

That is the extent of the case study. We now ask the participants to identify as many positive characteristics, traits, talents, and skills they can identify in 20 seconds. This first part of the exercise requires treasure hunting. Here is a sampling of the descriptive responses:

- responsible
- creative
- artistic
- athletic
- good speller
- persistent
- debater
- good brother
- advocate
- punctual
- honest
- sincere
- concerned
- energetic
- curious

This is just a sampling of the responses. We did not offer many positive expressions to describe Timmy, yet the Treasure Hunters discovered a good number of positive attributes in only 20 seconds. Note also that this exercise involved several participants; one person would not be able to identify so many of Timmy's assets and strengths. Together, though, our list grew substantially. This supports the *ME* to *WE* culture. When we engage more caring adults in a child's life, offer more Aces, and search for more treasures together, more children are afforded the opportunity to succeed. The following is a wonderful and true story of treasure hunting.

How to Find a Treasure

Most of Arizona is beautiful. One not-so-beautiful part lies a little south of Tucson. If you were to drive through this rocky, desolate area, you wouldn't give it a second thought— unless you believed there something special hidden in "them thar" hills. In 1974, two amateur weekend treasure hunters, Randy Tufts and Gary Tenen, made the discovery of a millennium. These two spelunkers spent countless hours in the arid desert. What kept their interest in an area many would not even set foot upon, let alone explore year after year, was their sixth sense that something special was hidden. Even after many disappointments in not finding their treasure, Tufts and Tenen did not give up.

It was one of those days when they were coming up empty handed. Exhausted, they were to pack it in when everything became very quiet; it was so quiet that they heard a strange sound. They turned toward it; what they were hearing was the earth taking a breath. They followed the breathing of the earth and found a sinkhole. They climbed into the sinkhole and there it was—Mother Nature's art studio.

Even more incredible was the fact that they caught Mother Nature working in her studio, creating her works of wonder. Stalagmites and stalactites merged to construct a 58-foot column of such beauty it was no wonder the earth took a breath; it, too, could not contain its emotion.

Tufts and Tenen understood what a powerful treasure they had discovered.

Today, Kartchner Caverns is a place of awe and beauty, where the spirit of the impossible is found. What makes this place so unique is that Mother Nature has decided to remain and continue her work. Many of her other studios have been so disturbed that she had to abandon them. To respect Mother Nature, Kartchner Caverns allows only 500 visitors a day, all of whom must pass through three sets of doors so as not to bother the artist.

Much of what we learned from Tufts and Tenen holds true for educators and youth workers. Sometimes after trying everything and nothing has worked—though they might be ready to give up—the treasure hunters keep digging. Treasures are sometimes hidden in locations unattractive on the outside. They aren't easy to find, and sometimes they exhaust even the strongest. But those who believe there is a treasure are rewarded if they do not give up.

And as we discovered from Tufts and Tenen, it helps to be very quiet. Listen for the breathing. Each breath hints that there is a treasure ready to be found. Mother Nature will not disappoint. She never has.

Chapter Fourteen

Top Five Practice #4
Passport to the Future

Universal Truth Number Three notes that kids succeed when they are able to articulate their future. When we speak about future, we focus on four destinations: home and family, education and career, community and service, and hobbies and recreation. By doing so, we offer definition to all efforts on behalf of children. These include supporting youth academically, socially, emotionally, physically, and spiritually during their development. The overall goal is to adequately prepare them for the journey from childhood to responsible adulthood.

In order to support this concept, we need to teach youth how to mentally time travel. Like teaching reading, math, science, art, riding a bike, driving a car, tying shoes—learning to mentally time travel requires a process. (See discussion in Chapter 3)

To help in that regard we created a "Passport to the Future," a simple but powerful instrument that helps guide the process of mental time travel. The idea of the "Passport to the Future," can be done by simply adopting the following process.

The Passport to the Future needs to be an age-/grade-appropriate instrument designed to help students recognize their past, understand their present, and prepare for their future. This process is called mental time travel. The ability to learn to time travel leads to hopefulness. *Hope is the ability to visit the future, return to the present, and prepare for the journey.*

When my granddaughter was three years old, she told me that when she grows up she is going to go to work like her mommy and daddy. I also recall her saying one day she was going to have a car like my mommy. She was beginning to mentally time travel.

Beyond the most obvious question that supports time travel, "What do you want to do when you grow up?," there is a list of equally important questions children need to hear. By expanding the number of questions asked and using the four destinations to frame them, we establish that the future is multidimensional. The following is a set of sample questions:

Home and Family (sample questions)

- Where do you want to live when you grow up?

- Do you want to live by the ocean, in the mountains, by a lake, where it snows, in the desert, on an island, in a big city, small city, farm, ranch, or somewhere else?

- Do you want to live in Rome, Paris, London, New York, Los Angeles, or Hortonville, WI?

- Do you want to live in a one-story home, a two-story home, a mansion, a farm, a ranch, a beach house, a city apartment, or a condominium?

Can you imagine anything more empowering for children than to believe they can control their own destiny? Just by asking such simple questions, we are empowering children with the gift of hope. The following are additional sample questions that explore these important destinations:

Home and Family (continued)

• Do you see yourself married?

• How many children do you want to have?

• One, two, three, four or more? How many boys or girls would you like to have?

• Do you see yourself as a good husband, wife, mom or dad?

• What do you see yourself doing for fun with your children?

Education and Career (sample questions)

• What would you enjoy studying after high school?

• Where would you like to go to school? In state or out of state?

• Would you like to study in another country?

Note that even if students struggle with the destination or associated questions, it is important to have them list something specific. One student told me that he didn't know if he was going to go to college or even finish high school. I asked him to do me a favor. I asked him to write down these three letters: A - S - U. These letters stand for Arizona State University. I said we would love to have him attend ASU.

I don't know if he will finish high school or go to college or attend ASU. What I do know is before our discussion, none of these thoughts were part of his thinking. My goal was to teach him to mentally time travel. For the first time he had a specific goal related to education and career. I also shared my belief that he could accomplish that goal.

Adults are responsible for helping all children articulate their future—to teach children to mentally time travel. There are *no exceptions* to that responsibility!

The following is another set of questions to consider in exploring a child's future.

Community and Service (sample questions)

• Whom do you want to help when you grow up?

• Do you want to help homeless people, starving people, or raise money to find a cure for a disease?

• Do you want to run for public office or coach a little league team?

• Do you want to help animals or the environment?

• Do you want to build a house for a needy family?

Hobbies and Recreation (sample questions)

This destination is a challenge for the adult and the child. Most children know what they enjoy doing as children for fun. Most have hobbies. This experience, however, is not a reiteration or restatement of their current hobbies and recreation. This destination allows children to empower themselves and think about what they can do for fun as adults that they can't do as children.

For example, when my then-15-year-old son said he wanted to go bungee jumping, I replied, "Over my dead body!" As an adult and a dad, I have the power and responsibility to determine what is appropriate for my son. But when my son became an adult, he was empowered and responsible for his own decisions. At age 25, he went bungee jumping. He didn't have to ask dear old dad.

Have children think beyond what they are currently doing for fun and relaxation, and to enjoy the overall quality of life.

- What do you want to do for fun when you grow up that your parents won't let you do now?
- Have you ever thought of learning to

  - fly fish;
  - horseback ride;
  - sky dive;
  - pilot a plane;
  - surf;
  - hike the tallest mountain in the world;
  - visit Paris, or Rome, or Hong Kong;
  - water ski;
  - learn to paint, cook, build a car;
  - design clothes;
  - hunt;
  - plant your own garden; or
  - remodel your home?

Each time you ask one of those questions, the brain pays attention and mental time travel is being taught and learned.

The following is an example of a letter to parents, teachers, and youth leaders of the our *Little Kids at Hope Passport to the Future* designed for pre-kindergarten—second grade:

To Parents, Teachers, and Youth Leaders,

Little Kids at Hope Passport to the Future is an exciting and interactive activity designed to help pre-kindergarten to second grade children begin to understand the concepts associated with goals and future and to ensure they feel bonded with adults.

A compelling body of evidence clearly demonstrates that children who understand the concept of goals and develop a sense of future better navigate life's challenges and opportunities than children who don't.

Additionally, it's widely known that children who feel loved, recognized, special, and successful within their relationships with caring adults grow up resilient and confident.

By introducing *Little Kids at Hope Passport to the Future*, Kids at Hope is creating an opportunity designed to prepare children for success.

Within its own research findings, Kids at Hope has identified the importance of defining one's future in terms of destinations. With the *Passport to the Future* framework, children will better understand that their future lies at home and family, education and career, community and service, and hobbies and recreation.

Following is an example of a letter to children.

Hi Girls and Boys,

We call this activity *Passport to the Future.* It's fun to pretend to see yourself as a grown up. You chose where you want to live, what you want to do for fun, whom you want to help, and what kind of job you would like to do.

Your *Passport to the Future* helps you thank the grown ups who love you and care so much about you. Those are just a few ideas to think about by using your *Passport to the Future.*

Have fun!

Again, the importance here is the conversation between adult and child in order to establish the conditions needed to process the time travel experience. The previously offered questions help in that regard.

A common concern about this process is judging whether goals are realistic. My short answer is that it is not the role of any adult including parents to judge a child's goals, as long as the goals are moral, ethical, and legal.

For example, many children see themselves as professional athletes. I congratulate them on that choice. Many adults impose their own sense of reality on children who have such a dream. They detail the astronomical odds against becoming a professional athlete. The strategy at Kids at Hope is much different. First, the problem is not with children who have unrealistic dreams, it is children who have no dreams at all, no hope at all. Even if outrageous, it is the child's dream.

The greater question is what to do about such lofty dreams. Here is where and how adults can guide the student through a series of goal-setting principles and action steps. Kids at Hope use their big dream to explore other options. For example, what do they want to do after their professional careers end? Do they want to coach, be a sports announcer, practice sports medicine, umpire, referee, own a team, or become a sports writer? We discuss being a great athlete and a smart athlete as well. The goal is to make sure children know they have options and that they can explore all of them.

The most important reason children need to understand the concept of options has to do with hopelessness, which can result when there are no longer options.

Adults create hope in children's lives. There are many strategies to support hopefulness in all children. We need to use as many of them as we can. Sharing the Passport to the Future is one of those strategies. The following story illustrates the power of using the Passport to the Future.

The Wizard of OZ
With a Little Bit of a Twist

The famous children's classic by L. Frank Baum, *The Wonderful Wizard of Oz* (1900), has withstood the test of time by sharing important values that continue to resonate generation after generation. Although there are many wonderful and colorful characters in the story, the three with whom we can all identify are the Cowardly Lion, the Tin Man, and the Scarecrow. Each lacks self-esteem; their futures seem bleak.

Upon becoming aware of these issues, the Wizard devises a set of novel solutions. He pins a hero's medal on the Cowardly Lion to validate his courage, he gives Tin Man a ticking clock to assure him that he does have a heart, and he hands the Scarecrow a diploma to certify his intelligence. Each character was enormously grateful to the Wizard. And yet, as we all know from the story, the receipt of the medal, ticking clock, and diploma only confirmed what was already there.

If we were to rewrite *The Wonderful Wizard of Oz*, we would add one more character, and like the other three, something would be missing. Without it, he would be challenged by a lack of purpose or value. This version would have a Child Without a Future. How would the Wizard help this child?

The Child Without a Future is not a fictitious character. He/she occupies homes, classrooms, youth organizations, recreation programs, and faith-based groups. This child is not invisible but may be ignored and anonymous. It's easy to not know his name because that takes time. It takes even more time to know her. He is easy to dismiss. The Child Without a Future did not choose poverty or parents who abuse or neglect her. He did not choose adults who see him as "at risk" and miss the hope that could be his. This child did not choose to have a life without a future.

What would a wise Wizard do for this child? What creative answer would he find as powerful as the ones he found for his previous three visitors?

Rather than a hero's medal, ticking clock, or diploma, the Wizard gives our Child Without a Future a Passport to the Future. This powerful document reminds him that he has always had a future. Though the adults in her life forgot to tell her of her treasures, the Aces remind her that what she thought that she lacked was there all the time. That's what adults are supposed to do.

Each adult has the power to be a Wizard. Business leaders, parents, neighbors, youth leaders, must demonstrate the wisdom and insight to validate children and their futures. It would be nice to wait for a Wizard to figure it out for us, but we cannot wait. And, as in the Land of Oz, the Wizard was just a common person who, as Dr. Ann Masten, notes, performs ordinary magic. According to Dr. Masten, it's not the extraordinary efforts that make a difference in a child's life; it's the ordinary efforts practiced by caring adults.

We must demonstrate the importance of believing in children, connecting with them, and teaching them how to time travel. What could be more extraordinary and magical than that?

Chapter Fifteen

Top Five Practice #5

Tracking Aces

Universal Truth II states that children have a greater chance to succeed if they have meaningful and sustainable relationships with caring adults. We can't overstate the importance of that understanding. We also cannot overstate how little attention it gets.

Top Five Practice #5 encourages the tracking of Aces in order to determine whether children are forming meaningful and sustainable relationships with adults. If we accept the premise of Universal Truth II, we must be committed to tracking it. An old management adage states, "You can't manage what you don't measure."

We roll the dice every day when it comes to kids' futures. We cross our fingers, hoping that adults are connecting with students, but we do not actually monitor, validate, or document whether that is occurring.

Perhaps we don't track relationships because we are more invested in our programs and services. We assume that children automatically benefit from being in school or a youth program. Therefore, we track attendance, program enrollment, absences, unexcused absences, participation, and the like. Nowhere in those systems can we tell whether the children are benefitting from a meaningful relationship.

Yet, that is exactly what our studies tell us ultimately makes a difference. What we do is substitute programs, curriculum, and instruction for meaningful relationships.

This fact also underscores the difference between bureaucracy and culture: programs, services, curriculum, and instruction are found in the bureaucracy; relationships are within the culture.

To correct this omission, Kids at Hope has created the technology called *Aces Tracking*. Aces is a metaphor for the four types of relationships children need: the Ace of Hearts represents the unconditional love and support offered by parents; the Ace of Clubs identifies those other adults who know and care about the child; the Ace of Spades represents those special adults who believe in students, sometimes more than students believe in themselves—they measure children by potential rather than by behavior; the Ace of Diamonds symbolizes adults who create opportunities for children to succeed.

We must ask, "Did the child receive Aces? Yes or no?" We must determine what Aces children are receiving and from whom.

Organizations using the Aces Tracking System upload their class or membership roster onto a secured website that permits access only by teachers and other adults including support staff such as bus drivers and cafeteria personnel.

With this system in the culture, organizations have the information needed to help all children succeed. The traditional bureaucratic protocol would be to refer a student with behavioral issues to a school counselor, social worker, psychologist, assistant principal, or principal—based on their job descriptions—whether or not any of these people actually know the child. In utilizing Aces Tracking, the organization has access to those individuals who know the student best, so perhaps the bus driver or cafeteria employee would help during the intervention. The student may respond more positively to someone who truly knows and cares about her or him. Children respond more to what's written on an adult's heart than what is inscribed on a business card. The ultimate goal is about making a difference in a student's life, not about maintaining the bureaucracy.

Bureaucracies and cultures function differently. To know whether any child is being left behind, use Aces Tracking as part of your cultural practices.

Chapter Sixteen

Where's the Village?

Where do we go from here? We have examined the Three Universal Truths and Top Five Practices that are simply the framework to approach strategically and holistically our child and youth development efforts. We have looked at the organization's culture as the soil in which to plant these truths and practices. But beyond the organization, how do we create a community-wide culture connected by a similar strategy? To that end. we examine the often-used expression, "It takes a village to raise a child." Our next step is to visit the village to determine if the villagers are really interested in raising a child.

Where is this mythical village that is suppose to raise our children? When we say it takes a village to raise a child, is the village a schoolhouse, a neighborhood, a city, county, state, or country? We need to know where to go to find the village. And if we are fortunate to find the village who are the villagers we are planning to ask to raise the child? Are we asking all of them or just some of them? And as importantly, what is it exactly that the village and its villagers are suppose to do to raise a child?

The questions can go on forever, but the underlying answer is obvious: Raising a child is neither easy nor intuitive. It requires knowledge and understanding of child and youth development, brain and cognition studies, the role of nutrition in physical growth, and psychological and social phases. We must seek to understand the interconnections of all matters in a child's life and their interceding impact. No one institution (including the family) can do it alone. We create myriad agencies, departments, and programs to support the development of children. And somewhere in all that, we have a village—or do we?

We know much that we do not practice. We seem to have all the right pieces to this difficult puzzle of raising a human being. With all the public and private money we spend, you would think we would have better results. After a century and a half of public education, a century of youth development services, and more than a half a century of government intervention and prevention programs, we still have an unacceptable school drop-out problem. Too many children still join gangs, take drugs, escape through alcoholism, become pregnant, are locked up, or just go through life aimlessly. So what is not working?

Maybe the village needs to begin to act like a village. We raise children in silos. Institutions do not talk with each other; rather, they focus on their own missions and services. We are filled with good intentions but are short on being intentional. We are more focused on groups of children rather than individual children. We segment children and ignore the whole child. So how might we support the success of all children?

First, what is the *village*? Which groups are parts of the village? Starting neighborhood by neighborhood, bring all the related services around the table. Get all those who work with children to know each other. This could be profoundly powerful for those children who slip through the cracks. Invite parents, teachers, group leaders, business people, social service professionals, school bus drivers, food service personnel, custodians, and front office workers. If it takes a village, invite the village.

Offer training to empower villagers with practical research-based information that includes the Three Universal Truths and Top Five Practices. Again, good intentions are not enough; the village needs strategic intentional practices.

The following questions and answers succinctly describe the process required to empower the village.

Questions

- What is the village?

- Who are the villagers?

- What is expected of the villagers?

- Do the villagers need training to meet these expectations?

- What will be achieved by the village?

Answers

1. A *village* is anywhere children live.

2. *Villagers* are all caring adults who want to make a difference in the lives of children. This is not about what is written on their business cards but what's written on their hearts.

3. Villagers are *expected* to provide and promote a culture where all children can succeed, *No Exceptions!* To achieve that, we must ensure all children know we believe in

them, are willing to connect with them and will help them learn to time travel to their future. *Hope is the ability to visit your future (home and family, education and career, community and service, and hobbies and recreation), return to the present, and prepare for the journey.*

4. Villagers *need training to meet their expectations.* Human beings have very few instincts, if any; what we know we have learned. Offering all caring adults the opportunity to learn new knowledge and skills in support of all children is required.

5. The village *will be defined.* When the village acts like a village we have found that

   - children become much more optimistic;
   - children understand and model the concept of hope;
   - children learn and practice the power of self-fulfilling prophecy (belief system) of positive self-talk;
   - children learn and practice the personal strength-based inventory;
   - children's academic and emotional achievement matures;
   - adults learn and practice the power of the self-fulfilling prophecy to support a child's achievement;
   - adults learn and practice how to measure children's potential, not just their behavior (*Strengths Based Report Card*);
   - adults learn and practice how to instill hope in every child without exception (*Passport to the Future*); and
   - adults learn and practice the types of meaningful and sustainable relationships needed by children.

Chapter Seventeen

Happiest Place on Earth

With an understanding of a strategic cultural framework supported by a series of practices, we have a clearer understanding about who in the culture comprises the village and how they might behave as a community.

This chapter identifies those who can specifically create the strategic culture necessary to act like a village. Again, we explore another side of developing such a culture.

When you think of words or phrases to describe local schools or youth development organizations I'm curious if the expression, *the happiest place on earth* comes to mind. Maybe it does if you are discussing Disneyland. But would thinking about a school or youth group in such a way be too much of a stretch? Institutions that serve youth evoke a great number of images when it comes to their purposes and missions; some good, some bad. Some of the children served by schools and youth agencies as we suggested earlier do very well in their programs and classrooms, some average, and many—after a century and a half of public education, and a century of youth development services—continue to struggle.

When you read the thousands of different mission statements that define these groups and institutions would you likely find words such as *happy* or *fun* offered as descriptors? Why not? Shouldn't schools and youth programs be places of happiness and fun, or should they be places of seriousness where children's futures are measured only by tests or risk factors?

We can also explore this question from a different perspective. Why aren't these places the happiest place for children? They theoretically possess the three most basic key elements for that ideal environment to exist. First, they are places where kids get to be with their friends. Second, they are places where they learn about the world, gain new knowledge and skills in order to dream, grow, plan, and prepare for the future. And third, they are places where all youth, no exceptions, are surrounded by adults who believe in them, connect with them and help them time travel.

Did someone decide our schools and youth program shouldn't be places defined by happiness, fun, or hopefulness? Is the process of learning and youth development incompatible with happiness? Most importantly, do we even think about the term *happy* in regard to the groups and organizations serving children? Certainly, we have come to understand that happiness is also an expression of physical and psychological health. Children and adults who are happy perform better in school, community and at work, are absent less, are able to set and reach their goals, and achieve a greater sense of personal fulfillment in all aspects of their lives.

So the question remains, should we even consider that schools and youth development organizations include *happy* as part of their missions?

When Walt Disney envisioned the "happiest place on earth," it was more than a marketing ploy. He first had to believe that he could create such a destination. He also had to find a way to make that assertion come to life. Although there are many examples of why Disneyland and its sister properties sustain such a powerful expression, most people would agree much of it has to do with the culture Disney created and the people it hires. Disney learned that to create the happiest place on earth, he needed to find happy people. He understood that he could not train people to be happy. He sought people who were secure in their own lives, maintained a sense of optimism, were fully engaged in what they do, easy with smiles, genuine, and able to create an environment conducive to success.

For schools and youth agencies to become places where happiness, hopefulness, and success thrive, they first need to ensure that those who work for them are happy, hopeful, and successful. No one can give that which he or she does not have. That concept applies to all those within an organization's culture, not only teachers, counselors, youth development professionals, and administrators, but also school bus drivers, support staff, custodians and maintenance personnel—all are responsible for acting as villagers.

First, Disney defined his culture, then he created the bureaucracy to support it, not to replace it.

If we follow the thinking of cultural psychology, anthropology, and now business and management, all of which include the study and understanding of culture as a key factor in their fields, we conclude that child and youth development workers must attend to the diverse goals and often contradictory beliefs about children and their development challenges. That being said, we need to be much more imaginative in recruiting, hiring, and training personnel. Typically, we hire for credentials, qualifications, and experience. If a major goal of our organization is to harness the cultural dynamics along with the bureaucratic systems, we must also examine the beliefs of candidates for compatibility to the culture we are creating. That is exactly what Disney did so wonderfully and what the fields of child and youth development and education have yet to embrace.

I am always curious as to why people lose their jobs, whether by termination or choice. We know that they were hired because they met the requirements of credentials, qualifications, and experience. Many lost or left their positions when their value systems—defined by their beliefs—and their behavior did not align with the culture of the organization. Keep in mind that may include good people having to leave or choosing to leave the job because the culture was toxic for them. Failing to clearly define the type of culture we want creates a vacuum allowing less favorable cultures to root.

Schools and youth organizations wanting to explore belief statements and culture compatibility should consider the following questions as part of the interview and assessment of a candidate. (These suggested questions are subparts of the whole assessment and no single response should qualify or disqualify a candidate. They transmit a sense of candidates' personal commitment to children.)

1. **If you were an organization of one person what would be your personal mission statement?**

   Listen to determine if the personal mission statement includes a mention of children.

2. **On a scale of 1 to 10, one representing strongly disbelieve/disagree and 10 strongly believe/agree, what number represents your view: All children are capable of success no matter what.**

Listen for the following:

- *Do they ask what you mean by success? If they do, respond by stating, "Use whatever definition of success you think is most appropriate."*

- *After they have selected a number, ask how they defined success and why they chose such a number.*

- *Although this question offers a choice of answers from strongly disbelieve/disagree to strongly believe/agree there are actually only two answers: number "1" and number "10." Any other number suggests the candidate wants to hedge.*

3. What would you say is the strongest determining factor related to a child's success in life?

This seeks to discover if the candidate would choose a factor such as personal beliefs and relationships, quality of teaching and training, or demographics (i.e., family, economics, or ethnic culture).

The purpose of these questions is to go beyond the bureaucratic inquiries related to job experiences, credentials, and qualifications to beliefs, expectations, and personal and collective efficacy. A good interviewer could create many more questions that would explore the cultural side of the candidate's qualifications.

When successful, the places our children attend become the happiest places on earth for them and the adults who work and volunteer there.

Chapter Eighteen

Culture Scan

Asking the Right Questions

In Chapter 4, "Testing Our Beliefs by Checking Our Blood Pressure," we underscored the importance of asking those who work with children about their beliefs, specifically about their acceptance or rejection that all children are capable of success, no matter what. We were curious if the people who surrounded our children and worked most directly with them actually believed in their potential to succeed. Our findings were not at the level we had hoped. Only 53% strongly believed all children are capable of success. That is disconcerting, because our research found that children have a greater chance of success when surrounded by adults who believe they will succeed. We obviously aren't there yet.

The following is our 11-question Culture Scan Survey, which seeks to compare people's beliefs with the practices of their organizations.

1. Default Section

1. Do you believe all students are capable of success no matter what.

	1 Strongly disagree/disbelieve	2	3	4	5	6	7	8	9	10 Strongly agree/believe
On a scale of 1-10 "1" representing strongly disagree/disbelieve up to "10" representing strongly agree/believe check the number which best represents your feelings or belief.	○	○	○	○	○	○	○	○	○	○

2. Do you believe that some students may not succeed due to negative family, social, or other environmental influences?

	1 Strongly disagree/disbelieve	2	3	4	5	6	7	8	9	10 Strongly agree/believe
On a scale of "1-10" similar to the first question please check the number which best represents your feeling or belief.	○	○	○	○	○	○	○	○	○	○

3. Do you believe that every person employed (faculty, administrators, support staff) by your school or organization believes all students can succeed no matter what.

	1 Strongly disagree/disbelieve	2	3	4	5	6	7	8	9	10 Strongly agree/believe
Similiar to the previous questions please check the number which best represents your feelings or belief.	○	○	○	○	○	○	○	○	○	○

4. Do you believe that other adults (parents/neighbors/business owners/workers) within your attendance area/community believes that all students can succeed no matter what.

	1 Strongly disagree/disbelieve	2	3	4	5	6	7.	8	9	10 Strongly agree/believe
Similiar to the previous questions please check the number which best represents your feeling or belief.	○	○	○	○	○	○	○	○	○	○

5. Do you believe it is a priority of your school that each student have a meaningful relationship with a teacher, administrator or other staff

	Strongly disagree/disbelieve									Strongly agree/believe
Similar to the previous questions please check the number which best represents your feeling or belief	○	○	○	○	○	○	○	○	○	○

6. What percentage of students in your school do you believe have a meaningful relationship with a teacher, administrator, and/or staff member?

○ Less than 20%

○ 21-40%

○ 41-60%

○ 61-80%

○ Over 80%

7. What percentage of students in your school do you believe will succeed as an adult?

○ Less than 20%

○ 21-40%

○ 41-60%

○ 61-80%

○ over 80%

8. What percentage of students in your school do you believe are hopeful and excited about their future?

○ Less than 20%

○ 21-40%

○ 41-60%

○ 61-80%

○ over 80%

9. Is goal setting taught to students in your school?

□ Yes

□ No

□ I don't know

---

10. If your school teaches goal setting which areas are its primary focus (select all that apply)?

☐ School work

☐ home and family

☐ Career

☐ Hobbies and recreation

☐ Future Education

☐ Serving community

☐ None of the above

11. Overall, I believe our administrators, teachers, staff and students feel that our school is a place where all students can experience success.

	Strongly disbelieve/disagree									Strongly believe/agree
On a scale of 1-10 please select the score which best represents your feelings.	○	○	○	○	○	○	○	○	○	○

Case Study

Belief and Practices
Culture Scan Survey
(Pre Culture Scan Survey)
Date of Report: October 27, 2011

Note: This survey represents the responses from 28 participants. Overall, this sample appears small but is representative of 85% of the faculty of an elementary school of approximately 300 students. The following is their report.

We have reviewed the data collected from our recent Culture Scan Survey of_____. As you recall, this survey has been designed to take a snapshot of the current attitudes and beliefs of your staff in relation to some of the practices research tells us are crucial to establishing a positive culture where all students can succeed, no matter what.

Purpose of the Culture Scan Survey

Youth Development advances a cross-, inter-, and transdisciplinary body of evidence that offers a greater understanding about success and failure. Those key elements/findings have become the basis for defining a cultural strategic framework designed to create and support an environment wherein all children can succeed, no matter what.

Therefore, the purpose of this survey is to identify beliefs and practices of individuals and organizations who share the responsibility for children's education, social, and emotional welfare and measure those beliefs and practices against research findings. Because personal and group attitudes affect collective efficacy, we can use these results in creating a culture that will affect a child's development and capacity to overcome adversity (resiliency) and achieve success.

In reviewing the survey data, it is important to keep in mind the three most prominent findings offered throughout the research include themes—Universal Truths (found universally throughout research and universal in terms of the application for children)—upon which this survey is based. These findings include the following:

1. **Children succeed when surrounded by adults who believe they will succeed.**

   Known as the Pygmalion Effect, self-fulfilling prophecy, subliminal priming and attribution theory, a half-century of research confirms that adults' attitudes and beliefs about children affect them, positively and negatively. The powers of adults' beliefs in children are consequential and must be examined to ensure all children are offered the opportunity to succeed.

2. **Children succeed when they have meaningful and sustainable relationships with caring adults.**

   Powerful and incontrovertible evidence exists that children who are connected with caring adults through meaningful and sustainable relationships do much better than children who are not. This simple understanding is, however, rarely documented or monitored. Do we truly know which of our children have meaningful and sustainable relationships with caring adults? Is it a priority of our schools, communities, and organizations that children feel connected?

3. **Children succeed when they are able to articulate their future.**

   Recent science defines this capacity to mentally explore one's future as being hopeful. Hope is shown to improve attendance, increase credits earned, lead to a higher grade point average; and increase a sense of well-being, happiness, and healthfulness. Most importantly, hope is not related to native intelligence or income and is malleable. Our interest concerns the intentionality of teaching *hopefulness.*

Survey Design

A cross-sectional analysis of baseline data was collected. Most answers were quantified on a 10-point Likert Scale or common interval-based multiple-choice style of question.

Findings and Conclusions

Question 1: Do you believe all students are capable of success, no matter what?

This question is designed to determine what percent of your organization truly believes all children are capable of success, no exceptions.

If respondents do not circle "10," why not? What prevents the adults in a child's life from believing all children can succeed, no exceptions?

Your Findings

- 57.1% selected number "10."

In order to represent school as a place where all adults believe all students can succeed, no exceptions, the goal over the next three years is for 80% or more to respond at a 10. Almost 43% are finding reasons some children cannot succeed.

Question 2: *Do you believe that some students may not succeed due to negative family, social, or other environmental influences?*

When we ask if all students can succeed, no matter what as noted in question 1, even those who face adversity, we find that those who scored high in their personal belief, tend to back off those beliefs when offered a possible reason or reasons why some children may not succeed. This tells us that even though adults want to believe (as shown in their responses to question 1), when presented with "at-risk" factors, many may find reasons some students will not succeed. In other words, many adults accept suggested reasons why some children may not succeed.

- When the "at-risk" factors are introduced, only 3.6% are able to maintain the highest belief. This compares to 57.1% responding in the affirmative (a "10") in question 1. (*Note that for question 2, a response of "1" is the same as a response of "10" in question 1.*)

The goal should be to achieve a similar response to both questions 1 and 2, indicating a strong belief in children's ability to succeed, no matter what. The goal for the results for question 2 would be 80% of the respondents awarding a "1," indicating a belief that all children can succeed even when faced with adversity. Establishing and holding to those beliefs strengthens the organization's culture.

Question 3: *Do you believe that every person employed (faculty, administrators, support staff) by your school or organization believes all students can succeed, no matter what?*

- Results revealed that 3.8% of respondents felt "very strongly" answering "10"; their fellow employees believed all students can succeed, no exceptions.

Again the goal is for 80% of the respondents to answer 10 or "strongly agree." Those results would indicate that each employee senses that their colleagues believe the way they do. That is not currently the case. Many of those who believe all students can succeed feel they are alone in their belief. The goal here is to build collective efficacy, a key factor in creating a strong positive culture.

Question 4: *Do you believe that other adults (parents, neighbors, business owners, workers) within your attendance area/community believe that all students can succeed, no matter what?*

- Expanding the sphere of influence reveals that 7.4% responded "very strongly" or "10," indicating a belief that people outside the school, including parents, feel the same way respondents do about their/your students.

These results are typical, especially in the Pre-survey: We tend to operate in silos. However, moving from good to great requires breaking down the silos. We need to find ways to engage parents and the community-at-large in establishing shared beliefs, principles, and practices in order to work toward the desired results. Kids at Hope defines this process as moving from *me* to *we*, which is critical in defining and building a culture. This expression helps us to better understand what is meant by "It takes a village to raise a child." The village must share a common belief about its children if it expects to help raise children. Consistency in responses to the first four questions would indicate progress in defining culture both in and out of school (community).

Question 5: *Do you believe it is a priority of your school that each student has a meaningful relationship with a teacher, administrator, or other staff?*

When exploring the notion of the school placing a high priority on students connecting (having meaningful relationships) with adults on campus, a strong majority felt that their school supports that value as a priority.

- 85.7% were able to rate their answer as a "10."

The goal is to have 90% of the respondents answering "10," suggesting the school/organization has made this a focused priority. Research is clear about children who have meaningful and sustainable relationships with caring adults being more capable of success than children who are disconnected or feel they are anonymous. Institutions and organizations serving children need this as a high priority as part of defining a culture.

Question 6: *What percentage of students in your school do you believe have a meaningful relationship with a teacher, administrator, and/or staff member?*

- 53.5% of respondents felt that less than 80% of the students were connected to someone at school in a meaningful way.
- 17.8% felt less than 60% were connected to someone at school in a meaningful way.

The goal would be that 90% of respondents would believe and know that over 80% of students would indeed be meaningfully connected to someone at school. If it is a priority of the school (see question 5), steps should be taken in order to insure that responses, more importantly, actual practice be consistent with the perception. What we are seeking to understand is, do the belief and practice match up?

> *Question 7:* *What percentage of students in your school do you believe will succeed as adults?*

This question is designed to once again test the commitment to one's belief and the power of the self-fulfilling prophecy.

Does what we learn, especially in question 1, match the learning from question 7? If not, why not? In the case of Mills Parole, the match is interesting suggesting those who believe all children can succeed, no exceptions is consistent with their answers in this question.

- 50% believe over 80% of students in their school will succeed as adults.

Eighty percent of respondents should be able to answer that they believe 80% or more of their students will succeed as adults. Addressing this should be a priority.

> *Question 8:* *What percentage of students in your school do you believe are hopeful and excited about their future?*

- Responses reveal that 39.3% of the adults believe that over 80% of students are hopeful and excited about their future.
- 21.4% answered that less than 60% of the students are hopeful and excited about their future.

Research is consistent about the importance of children's ability to articulate their future and the connection to hope and well-being. We need to work toward creating a culture where over 90% of the adults know that 80% or more of the students are hopeful and excited about their future. A student's sense of hope and excitement is directly related to adults who are part of a child's life.

Question 9: *Is goal setting taught to students in your school?*

- 85.7% believed goal setting is taught.
- 10.7% said it isn't taught.
- 7.1% did not know.

This is a common disconnect. Everything taught and learned in our schools and after-school programs is about the future, and the future is about setting goals. If students cannot connect what they learn in school to their future then our efforts lose their impact. The goal here is to create a culture supported by practices that demonstrate that what is learned in school is helpful to succeeding at life's four destinations: home and family, education and career, community and service, hobbies and recreation. Formal education and youth development activities (knowledge, skills, characteristics, and experiences) taught and offered empower students to succeed.

Question 10: *If your school teaches goal setting, which areas are its primary focus?*

- 96.0 % schoolwork
- 76.0 % future education
- 48.0% career
- 32.0 % family
- 20 % serving the community
- 20% state hobbies and recreation

While it is understandable that an educational institution would have education and career as its primary focus, students need to understand that life's journey is multidimensional and requires guidance in more than those areas. The concept that life's journey is also about home and family, community and service, hobbies and recreation, and education and career must be developed and nurtured. When students are emotionally connected to their education by recognizing that what is learned will help them in four destinations, not to just pass a test, earn a grade (school work), or get a job (career), more students will succeed.

If you are a community-based organization, are your results showing a balance?

Question 11: *Overall, I believe our teachers, administrators, staff, and students feel that our school is a place where all students can experience success.*

- 50% strongly agree/believe in the aforementioned statement

As with most of the previous questions, the goal is to have 80% of all respondents answer a "10" or "strongly agree/believe."

Summary

We find your employees wanting to believe all students can succeed, no exceptions. They aren't there yet and lack the evidence that a culture is in place that supports that belief.

Again, the most critical finding we discovered through this Culture Scan Survey is that most schools are organizationally but not yet culturally focused. Policies are in place, but beliefs and practices around those beliefs are not firmly established. What we know for a fact is institutions/organizations that focus only on systems but not on culture may operate efficiently but not effectively. It is the culture that determines the effectiveness—the *want-tos*; whereas the organization systems (i.e., bureaucracy) establish the *have-tos*.

To achieve a culture where we believe and practice all children are capable of success, no exceptions, we must move from *me* to *we*.

Thank you for your participation!

Chapter Nineteen

The Anne Fox Elementary School Miracle

We started this book with a simple premise; either you believe all children are capable of success no matter what, or you don't. If you do, we can move on and create a world where all children can succeed. If you don't, we have to move on without you because your commitment to your belief may be emotional and that is impossible to change. What schools and organizations need to accept is the fact that some personnel are unable to change due to their emotional investment in their beliefs. Therefore, there is no reason to quarrel with or become frustrated because of it. What needs to be acknowledged is the acceptance that only change can improve the future for millions of children who are too easily written off. Some adults will be unable to accept and support that decision. We have been held hostage for too long to those unable to believe in all our children without exception.

Anne Fox Elementary School near Chicago understood that. Here is their story as told by Annette Acevedo in a doctoral dissertation (2009) while a student at Roosevelt University, Chicago, Illinois.

Dr Acevedo's challenge was to describe and explain the beliefs and practices of Anne Fox Elementary School in Hanover Park, Illinois, that went from the worst academically performing school within a school district of 21 schools to the second top performing school in just a few years. Since Dr. Acevedo's study, Anne Fox became the top performing school in the district.

How did such a remarkable transformation occur? It began with a belief.

The purpose of this study was to describe and explain the practices employed to improve student performance within an elementary school, grades K-6, as new leadership emerged and as changes in instructional practices, norms, and beliefs were enacted. Practices incorporated over a period of several years were investigated and described primarily from the voices of the school principal and a lead teacher, although the perspectives of classroom teachers/staff were included also. The school of study was situated in a working-class and ethnically diverse community of about 38,000 residents near Chicago. There were seven school districts that fell within the boundaries of the town. The racial/ethnic make up, as categorized by the U.S. Census Bureau (2000) fact sheet was approximately 68% White, 28% Hispanic, 12% Asian, 6% Black, and 10% other. According to the 2008 Illinois school report card, the demographics of the school and district were as follows, respectively (percentages have been rounded up): 33/52% White, 11/7% Black, 25/18% Hispanic, 15/19% Asian/ Pacific Islander, 7/4% Multiracial/ethnic, 24/12% low income, 22/13% limited-English proficient and 8/12% mobility rate. The total enrollment for 2008 was close to 400. Although these figures may not appear to be staggering numbers when compared to other suburban districts or urban schools, the differences were more significant when compared to the averages of this district in general. For instance, the school's low-income rate was double the district's rate, and its mobility rate has also fluctuated through the years, at times being double that of some schools in the district or higher than the districts average.

During the 2005-2006 academic school year, when the acting principal assumed the school's leadership position, it was the lowest achieving school in the district (21st out of 21 schools in terms of academic performance). The distinction of being the lowest performing school in the district earned it the "at-risk" label. Additionally, the fact that the school's demographics were not similar to most of the other schools in the district, entrenched further the notion of "at risk." If nothing else, the difference in demographics allowed for an "easy" explanation of causation of the problem with low achievement.

In spite of the labels and the school's history, the students made remarkable academic growth in the past three years under the leadership of a new principal, per a review of the state report cards. The overall performance of the state standardized test (Illinois Standards Achievement Test-ISAT), combining all tests, showed an increase of 25 percentage points for students meeting or exceeding state standards from 2005 to 2008. In 2005, 69% of the students met that mark; in 2006, 79% did; in 2007, 89% did; and by 2008, 94% of the student body was reaching the benchmark of either "meets" or "exceeds." This showed that the formerly most "at-risk" school of the district was now functioning above the district's level of 89% and exceeding the number of the state where

79% of students reached the "meets" or "exceeds" benchmarks. Because of these improved academic gains, a seemingly improved culture from within, and a more positive perception from the community, this study examined the many practices that led to the remarkable turnaround results of the school. Consequently, this study helped extend research on factors that promote academic achievement, improved social-emotional functioning, and overall student success, in general.

Questions Guiding the Study

The specific questions guiding the study were as follows:

1. What systemic elements need to be in place in a school to establish the foundation for improved student achievement?

2. How do teachers ensure that mechanisms of resiliency, hope, and a belief system of high expectations lead to greater student achievement and success?

Among a number of findings and conclusions offered by Dr. Acevedo was the realization that understanding the collective perceptions of a group required establishing a sense of collective efficacy was an understudied area. She notes, ". . .given that no general body of theory has been produced to explain practices that lead to improved student achievement in a school culture that heightens performance by building hope, optimism, and resiliency in youth, a mixed approach was taken to collect data for this study."

Dr. Acevedo's conclusions helps us to better understand how culture is created when mastery experiences increase among teachers particularly when they learn from one another, believe in their own efficacy and that of their colleagues, and enjoy their job more because of it. She found, as we did, that as "teachers' perceptions as a whole—that they could teach students successfully and attain positive outcomes—resulted in higher student achievement at the school."

The *Refined Conceptual Framework* designed by Dr. Acevedo (see Figure 19.1) to describe the "influence of perceived collective efficacy beliefs in high needs schools" reminds us that there is no substitute for visionary leadership to create a cultural strategy based on two overriding constructs: academic high expectations and a

Figure 19.1. Refined Conceptual Framework

belief system that stated *all children are capable of success, no exceptions. Environmental factors* including teacher efficacy, professional learning communities and instruction and *empowerment factors* including learned optimism, resiliency (protective factors), and social emotional competence—all supported this overall strategy.

Through this study we can understand the dynamics required to foster collective efficacy and how it can be channeled to accomplish high academic goals.

As importantly we can also see something as consequential—the adults at Anne Fox Elementary School fostering among each other a greater sense of hopefulness, optimism, and success. Yes, the students succeeded, and the adults did too. We mustn't forget that.

I've been to Anne Fox Elementary School many times. Kids at Hope has conducted its series of trainings for the school and over the years has had representatives attend our annual Youth Development Master's Institute. Additionally, our national board of directors also visited the school to witness first hand the transformation and learn directly from the administrators, the mayor of Hanover Park, parents, teachers, and students. We continue to learn from Anne Fox as they do from us.

One of the personal lessons I have taken from the Anne Fox story is about leadership. I have had the pleasure of visiting close to 1,000 educational and youth development leaders throughout my career. All started their professional journey on the low rungs of a ladder. The ones I have had the opportunity of visiting are now principals, superintendents, executive directors, or presidents of organizations.

Through these visits, exchanges of ideas and strategies, and partnerships, I have come to appreciate the difference between good leadership and good management. No one would be surprised to learn that most of the people in these positions are very good managers. Very few are good leaders. Anne Fox is all about leadership.

Many schools and youth organizations find themselves in the same negative spiral that Anne Fox was in prior to 2005. Many schools and youth groups are still there. Others are not as dire as Anne Fox was, but they are far from achieving comparable success. The reason is simple: They lack the belief and commitment. I speak to people every day who are in leadership positions but function more as managers. This is what I hear:

- We don't have the time.
- We don't have the money.
- We don't mandate change from a central office.
- We are focused on instruction rather than the whole child.
- We can't add anything more to the plate of our staff.
- We do our own thing at this school.
- We don't have problems at our school.
- I'll let my staff decide if they want to do it.
- We're different here.

I have also benefitted from transformative leaders whose focus in on the whole child. The conversation is much different. Here are their statements:

- I always have time to learn about helping children succeed
- Where there's a will, we will find the way

- We may not mandate from the central office, but we do lead

- We are focused on the whole child because children grow up holistically.

- We aren't looking to add to our already-filled plate, but we are interested in finding a stronger plate.

- We want to be part of something larger than just the four walls of our organization.

- We are concerned about every child in our school

- I was appointed to lead this organization to decide and, most importantly, to understand what's important for all our children

- Every child needs to know adults believe in them, connect with them, and help them learn to see and plan for their future.

- We understand the difference between bureaucracy and culture.

It's difficult to understand what prevents a school, youth organization, and an entire community from demonstrating that they believe all children can succeed, No Exceptions; that they are willing to make a commitment to ensure children feel connected to caring adults; and that they are willing to help all youth learn to see a future filled with opportunity, hope, and success at four destinations. The only answer I can come up with that prevents them from such a commitment is they *don't* believe all children can succeed; they are *unwilling* to focus on the types of relationships children require; and *fail* to grasp the importance of teaching children about time travel.

Chapter Twenty

What We Know, What We've Learned

We've covered much ground exploring the difference between kids succeeding and those struggling. We've attempted to outline the most profound recurring evidenced-based findings into a simple strategic framework that serves as a mental blueprint for all caring adults' efforts on behalf of children. This blueprint establishes a conscious strategy consisting of Three Universal Truths and Five Top Practices that when believed and practiced positively affect each child's and youth's opportunity for success:

Universal Truth I: Children succeed when surrounded by adults who believe they can succeed.

Universal Truth II: Children succeed when they have meaningful and sustainable relationships with caring adults (Aces).

Universal Truth III: Children succeed when they can articulate their future at four destinations (mental time travel).

These truths thrive in a culture not a bureaucracy. If not believed, these truths cannot be effectively practiced. If they are fully embraced then the following Top Five Practices are remarkably effective.

1. Celebrating and articulating the belief that all children can succeed, No Exceptions!

2. Practicing the power of self-talk

3. Ensuring that all children and youth receive a strength-based Report Card focused on their nonacademic strengths, talents, skills, characteristics, and traits

4. Offering every child and youth a Passport to the Future that teaches the brain about mental time travel

5. Tracking every child and youth's Aces, therefore ensuring no child is disconnected from the importance of meaningful and sustainable relationships with caring adults

In summary, we have created the following schematic that shows how thinking about child and youth development must evolve along with scientific findings.

Table 20.1 compares 20th Century Thinking and Practices against what we need in the 21st Century to help all children succeed.

Table 20.1

Rethinking Child and Youth Development and
Education Strategies

20th Century Thinking	21st Century Thinking
Mission Driven	Shared Beliefs
Program focused	Relationship focused
Studying Risk	Studying hope, resiliency, assets and strengths
Bureaucracy as change agent	Culture as change agent
Focus on Job Descriptions	Focus on Shared Responsibilities
Success defined very narrowly	Success defined holistically

The Proof is in the Evaluations

Our pursuit of a better understanding of why some children succeed and others struggle led to Universal Truths (1993-1999). From there our early models led to identifying the Top Five Practices (1999-2005).

Throughout this process, we evaluated our efforts every step of the way. To date, six researchers have investigated the effectiveness of our strategy and practices. In addition to Annette Acevedo's study about Anne Fox Elementary School in Chapter 19, the following are highlights from other studies and evaluations.

As early as 1999, we knew we were on the right track. Baker and Martinez (1999) completed an evaluation of students who participated in our efforts against those organizations that did not. Participant ratings on two of the of five protective factor subscales—caring adults and sense of acceptance and belonging—were significantly higher than those who were not exposed to our strategy.

U.S. Department of Education Counseling Grant Evaluation

Over a three-year period (2001-2004), we were contracted by Dysart Unified School District in Arizona who had received a U.S. Department of Education Counseling Grant. Our goal was to create a positive school climate/culture of success for all students, without exception. In order to meet this lofty expectation, the district had Kids at Hope train all employees, certified and noncertified, within the cultural belief system and strategies.

According to the Arizona Prevention Resource Center, an Arizona State University entity, the following results were defined:

1. Increase in school attendance
2. Students learned to deal with their feelings
3. Students achieved a sense of empowerment
4. Students increased their self-confidence
5. Increased secondary aspirations; younger children can set goals and are aware of careers
6. A peaceable environment was created; 270 fights were recorded in one year. The fights dropped to 30 the following year; nine students were in detention on average each year (during the study period) and dropped to only four to five in subsequent years.

Additionally, the report cites that 90% of the teachers surveyed indicated that we had a positive impact on their school environment and students. The study underscored "By training all staff, the culture of the program was developed. The foundation was established for improving the school climate for all students, teachers, staff, and parents."

A bus driver who had been trained noted that he began to understand the importance of being the first school official to greet the children each day and saw his role as responsible in setting the tone. The bus driver noted that he practiced what he had learned through Kids at Hope and witnessed much less disruptive behavior on his bus.

U.S. Department of Education Grant
Performance Evaluation

In 2003, we formed a partnership with Blueprint Education promoting the cultural framework. The belief system and strategy was subsequently adopted by a new charter high school in Phoenix, Arizona. The school was born of the belief system that all students can succeed, *no exceptions!* The goal at Hope Academy is to teach all students effectively, especially children living in poverty. External evaluator, Dr. Nancy Haas, Department Chair, Secondary Education, Arizona State University at the West Campus, reviewed and summarized data collected as part of the U.S. Department of Education grant awarded to the high school. The data were judged to be both valid and reliable and included both quantitative and qualitative information. The overall finding strongly suggested that the administration, faculty and staff are committed to improving student achievement and overall success of the students.

Study of Five Schools

Students attending five schools of which at least one staff member has participated in our trainings completed surveys to determine if they had factors to promote their resilience. According to Dr Frances Bernat, with the School of Criminology and Criminal Justice at Arizona State

University and cited in the journal, Women and Criminal Justice (2009), "The results of this research show that youth who believe that they are successful and who are optimistic about themselves and their schools are more likely to find their schools to be places where they can be successful and optimistic."

Some of Bernat's most significant findings included the following:

- Female students reported doing better than their male counterparts in school.

- More female than male students felt their parents, teachers, and school police resource officers cared about them.

- Although male and female students appeared indifferent about bus drivers and after-school workers, more male students reported a less caring relationship with these individuals.

- Female students reported that their teachers had higher expectations for them; male students did not think their teachers had higher expectations for them.

According to Bernat:

In order to create a place of refuge, school culture needs to manifest the belief that all children are capable of success, no exceptions. This manifestation is reflected in a youth's identity as a kid at hope and in a belief that his or her school provides a place of hope. Significant correlations existed between a youth identifying himself or herself as a kid at hope and his or her school as a place of hope with various factors of resilience. Thus, the more youth believed that their school was a place where students got along with one another and teachers praised them and could help them to be better people, then the youth and the school were manifesting the core values of resilience: hope, optimism, and success. Although differences by race were significant, as noted above, teachers and schools that make a concerted effort to engage the youth and provide a positive learning environment should see the racial differences abating.

We've come a long way discussing and examining a unique approach in the fields of child and youth development and education. We conclude that if we are consumed with the risk factors in our children, we will never unleash the potential in each young person we talk about but fall short of achieving. If we, however, start with a premise and commit to not abandoning it, that all children are capable of success regardless of what else is happening in their lives we become empowered in pursuit of that achievement.

Chapter Twenty-One

A Thought From Professor Einstein

This book with its concepts, theories, principles, and practices offers a different view of child and youth development and education. We abandoned conventional wisdom in pursuit of new thoughts to help us better understand the forces that determine a child's fate. Early on, we noted that Albert Einstein encouraged a different level of thinking to solve problems. We, therefore, chose to imagine how the good professor would have used his remarkable insights to better understand children and their potential. We conclude this book, then, by allowing Einstein to support our case.

Einstein taught us much about our universe. He was able to see the obvious in the invisible—no small accomplishment! In addition to his achievements in the world of science, most specifically physics, he had a deep understanding of humankind and human potential. For well over a century, scientists, philosophers, classroom teachers, and other mortals have been drawn to this sockless professor, who used poetic eloquence and simplicity to afford humankind a glimpse into the mind of the universe.

What was it about this 26-year-old assistant patent clerk, who had dropped out of high school, failed on his first attempt at entering college, and couldn't even find a job as a high school teacher that still permitted him to understand the creation of the universe? And, equally important, how can Einstein's most famous equation help us better understand the enormous energy and potential in all children? We explore a series of concepts drawn from Einstein's work for the purpose of establishing a theoretical equation that offers a greater understanding of our world's children and their place in our universe.

First let's try to understand what we know about the intelligence and potential of children. Over the centuries, learned individuals have argued about intelligence and capacity of the races that inhabit our planet. History is filled with the powerful relegating groups of people to inferior societal and economic positions Attempts have been made to prove racial, gender, ethnic, or socioeconomic stereotypes scientifically valid. Fortunately, sound science usually saves the day. Unfortunately for many, that day comes much too late. In today's enlightened industrial and technologically advanced society, remnants of these prejudices continue to manifest themselves with peculiar and damaging consequences. The most common of these attempts to diminish the capacity of one group over another is the use and abuse of the misguided expression, *youth at risk.*

After careful examination, we understand that children labeled as *at risk* often seem to be members of the same population groups previous generations tried to demean intellectually and socially. We continue to attempt to create new criteria so we can appear to be on solid scientific footing, only to find ourselves in the same quicksand as those who tried to impose their biases on us decades earlier.

When we study the criteria we have established for those we have identified as *at risk*, we devalue the intelligence and potential of certain groups and individuals of color, ethnicity, and socioeconomic backgrounds. So why do we continue to search for reasons, arguments, and facts to establish why some people or children do well intellectually, socially, and economically, and others don't? And why do the same individuals and groups continue to be identified as handicapped by circumstances such as social position, economic status, and even their parents' educational achievement, among others.

Einstein might participate in this discussion as he did for the world of physics, cosmology, astrophysics, nuclear physics, solid-state physics, space travel, and electronics. His presence enables us to relate his understanding about the workings of the universe to our knowledge about children. To engage the good professor we must understand how he concluded that $E=mc^2$.

The simplest answer to this most complex question can be found in the manner in which Einstein viewed his world. He had the uncanny ability to question everything and everybody, even the icons of the scientific world. "Imagination is more important than knowledge," he said, "for knowledge is limited to all we now know and understand, while imagination embraces the entire world, and all there ever will be to know and understand."

To know this side of Einstein, prepares us for this next insight: "All I have tried to do in my life is ask a few questions. Could God have created the universe any other way, or had he no choice? And how would I have made the universe if I had the chance?" It isn't surprising then that Einstein took on the scientific establishment and ushered in a new, more precise understanding of our universe. Part of a series of papers he wrote in 1905 was, "Does the Inertia of a Body Depend Upon its Energy Content?" He suggested that mass and energy were basically two sides of the same coin. The formula explains the dynamic relationship between energy and matter. The introduction of c^2 is the conversion factor explaining how the mass energy linkage operates (Bodanis, 2000).

The next question, then, is how much energy exists in mass? Einstein's answer is that it is almost beyond comprehension. Mass is any object or substance that can be determined by the weight on a scale or the amount of force necessary to accelerate it. Mass, then, is omnipresent in our universe and the amount of energy ready to explode from it is equal to the speed of light squared, multiplied by the object's mass. If someone weighs 150 pounds, you would then need to multiply that number by 448,900,000,000,000,000, which is the speed of light squared, or, as Einstein represented it, c^2. That would be enough energy to power a small city for a week, if only you could convert it (Moring 2000). So what is Einstein teaching us about children? First, children are, in fact, part of our universe. They contain mass, and as we have learned, mass converted into energy is enormous. However, human energy is converted into achievement. It's represented by our inherent capacity to contribute to those areas that improve our planet and our universe. Therefore, we represent our Theory of Human Potential by the equation $P=kc^2$.

As simply as Einstein's $E=mc^2$ equation represents our understanding of the universe and how it operates, we express understanding of children in a profound manner, with uncomplicated ease and grace so as to capture the enormous potential each child is capable of offering our world. Let us analyze the $P=kc^2$ principle. If energy and mass are manifestations of the same thing, regardless from where that mass is derived, and energy potential is always equal to itself multiplied by the speed of light squared, then our equation must represent that all children (k for kids) regardless of their ancestry, current conditions, gender, or any other conditions, real or imagined, possess an enormous amount of potential (P). We could argue that the laws of the universe would require us to apply c^2 to understand the quantity of potential, and we would probably be quite close. Our first challenge requires us to accept this equation, not necessarily as fact, but that it makes sense.

Einstein's work was essentially ignored when first published. It is difficult for many of us to abandon our thoughts and beliefs, even in the face of new evidence. But Einstein also taught us "We cannot solve today's significant problems at the same level of thinking we were at when we created them." Families, education and social service institutions are still searching for the tools that might release the enormous potential in all children, and convert it into positive achievement. But we cannot release that potential if we don't believe it exists in all children. Einstein taught us that energy exists in all matter, not just some.

At the end of the nineteenth century, scientists approached their questions as though nothing were connected to anything else. Some sought answers to the nature of light, the structure of the atom, the lack of ether, mass as separate from energy and so on. It took Einstein to connect the dots. We question whether we have returned or possibly never left the late 1800s. We continue to look at children through separate microscopes or telescopes, failing to connect the dots, and seeing parts of the problem. For example, do parents really engage with their children's teachers? Do our teachers collaborate with our preschool, before school, and after-school youth service organizations? Do youth service professionals really know what is going on in the schools and homes of the children they serve? The answer is a deafening "no!" Our children are shuffled from one theoretical framework and practitioner to another. "God does not play dice with the universe," Einstein stated. We agree! Furthermore, we do not believe God plays dice with children's potential. Unfortunately, we do.

Failure to recognize their potential and connect the dots reduces children's future to a roll of the dice. Some will make it and others will not. Committing to our children's success, No Exceptions, is one powerful factor that, if adopted, would ensure the release of a huge amount of every child's positive potential and convert it into achievement. But it has become much easier to blame, create stereotypes, and ignore the real issues than it is to offer all children the one factor they need to release their potential. At birth, babies have 100 billion neurons ready to connect. That is a lot of potential.

During the first three years of life, the nurturing process is critical to the creation of neural pathways to maturation of the brain and its potential. Unless parents are committed to understanding and practicing the stimulation their babies' brain need during this time, many of those neural pathways may never be created. During the first 18 years of a child's life, his/her brain, mind, spirit, intellect, and body develop rapidly. At each stage of this development—0-3 years of age, 4-6, 7-10, 11-14, and 15-18—the forces of nature are in place waiting to be triggered. That can happen only if the community is committed to releasing the potential of every child, without exception. Is there anything in Einstein's work that can help us understand the importance of commitment?

Yes, indeed. Let us return to the value of the speed of light squared and why in our universe such a value is so important. Firstly, squaring a number is something we understand mathematically in our physical laws. Secondly, once we discovered that the speed of light is the one absolute constant in our world, it is then a natural assumption to combine these two understandings to explain how even very little mass is magnified enormously when it emerges on the side of energy (Bodanis, 2000). In our social world, we must take advantage of that knowledge by recognizing that when we rally a community around children so that every child experiences the same level of commitment from many adults, then the concept of commitment is squared.

We believe that low social capital or social isolation (i.e., the lack of commitment a village makes to its children) is predictive of more illness, more crime in neighborhoods, less economic success, more violence, and less school success. Children cannot realize their full potential unless they have committed adults in their lives. Every caring and committed adult who becomes part of the child's development—a teacher, coach, minister, rabbi, youth or recreation worker, counselor, bus driver, school cafeteria worker, neighbor, or any of the thousands of adults who cross paths with our children during their first eighteen years—can contribute support. We define this as squaring our commitment to better explain how we can release the potential in all young people. This book draws on the universal knowledge.

In his article *Does the Inertia of a Body Depend on its Energy Content?* (1905), Einstein introduced the equation $E=mc^2$. By drawing upon his argument, we concluded that the laws of the universe also apply to children as they apply to mass and energy. Instead of trying to find reasons why some children succeed and others fail, we contend that first we must recognize that all children, regardless of their gender and social, economic, or ethnic, background or other factors, possess the same capacity to succeed and achieve if we are committed by our positive relationships with them to release the enormous potential each possesses, without exception.

Could our equation be as simple as Einstein's $P=kc^2$? P=Potential; K=Kid; C=individual commitment;

C^2=commitment from the community. Every Kid has Potential. How much of that potential is realized is a result of the individual's commitment and community's commitment to the child. We measure commitment on a scale from 1-10 (strongly disbelieve /disagree to strongly believe/ agree all children can succeed, no matter what.

It's a powerful conclusion and enormous responsibility to accept the fate of all our children by understanding it simply begins with whether or not we believe in them.

Thank you, Professor Einstein.

References

Acevedo, A. (2010). *The influence of perceived collective efficacy beliefs on student achievement: Increasing social-emotional factors to improve school culture and student success.* Ann Arbor, MI: ProQuest LLC.

Annie E. Casey Foundation KIDS COUNT Data Center. (2011). *Indicator Name.* Retrieved from datacenter.kidscount.org.

Applestein, C. (1998). *No such thing as a bad kid.* Gifford School Weston, MA.

Barber B. K., & Olsen, J. A. (1997). Socialization in context: Connection, regulation, and autonomy in the family, school and neighborhood, and with peers. *Journal of Adolescent Research 12(2):*287-315.

Battin-Pearson S., Newcomb, M. D., Abbot, R. D., Hill, K. G., Catalano, R. F., & Hawkins, J. D. (2000). Predictors of early high school dropout: a test of five theories. *Journal of Educational Psychology, 92(3):*568-582.

Baum, F. (1900). *The wonderful Wizard of OZ.* Chicago, IL: George M. Hill Company.

Bernat, F. (2009). Youth resilience: Can schools enhance youth factors for hope, optimism, and success? *Women in Criminal Justice, 19,* 251-256.

Bodanis, D. (2000). *E=mc2: A biography of the world's most famous equation.* New York: Berkley Publishing Group.

Calaprice, Alice (Ed.). (2000). *The expanded quotable Einstein.* Princeton University Press.

Carlos, John, & Miller, Rick. (2002). *Kids at hope: Every child can succeed, no exceptions.* Reston: American Association for Leisure and Recreation.

Children's Defense Fund, State of America's Children. (2011). Retrieved from www.childrensdefense.org/child...data.../ state-of-americas-2011.pdf

Clark, R. (1984). *Einstein: The life and times.* New York: Avon Books.

Collins, J., & Porras, J. (2009). *Built to last.* New York, NY: Harper Collins.

Comer, James. (1995). Lecture given at Education Services Center, Region IV, Houston, TX.

Gallup, Inc. (2010). *Overall Score Card-Spring 2010,* Retrieved from http://www.gallupstudentpoll.com/145517/Gallup-Scorecard-Overall-Spring-2010.aspx

Gabarino, J. (1995). *Raising children in a socially toxic environment.* San Francisco: Jossey-Bass.

Gardner, H. (1983). *Frames of the mind.* New York, NY: Basic Books.

Gibilisco, S. (1991). *Understanding Einstein's theories of relativity: Man's new perspective on the cosmos.* Mineola: Dover Publications.

Hawking, S. (December, 1999). A Brief History of Relativity. *Time,* 66-81.

Kids at Hope. (2006). *The science behind kids at hope.* Research Synthesis, Kids at Hope.

Klem A. M., Connell, J. P. (2004). Relationships matter: Linking teacher support to student engagement and achievement. *Journal of School Health, 74*(7):262-273.

Kornhaber, M. L. (2001). "Howard Gardner" in J. A. Palmer (Ed.), *Fifty modern thinkers* (p. 276).

Krauss, L. (August, 2006). Nice Going, Einstein, *Discover: Science, Technology, and The Future,* 38-39.

Kyunghwa, L., & Johnson, A. (2007). Child Development in Cultural Contexts: Implications of Cultural Psychology for Childhood Teacher Education. *Early Childhood Education Journal.* Retrieved From Academia.edu http://sc.academia.edu/Amyjohnsonlachuk/Papers/384678/Child_Development_in_Cultural_Contexts_Implications_of_Cultural_Psychology_for_Early_Childhood_Teacher_Education

Masten, A. (2009). Ordinary Magic: Lessons from research on resilience in human development. *Education Canada, 49*(3): 28-32. http://www.cea-ace.ca/media/en/Ordinary_Magic_ Summer09.pdf http://www.pbs.org/thisemotionallife/blogs/ ordinary-magic

Maurer, R. (2004). One small step can change your life. New York, NY: Workman Publishing Company.

Mayo Foundation for Medical Education and Research (MFMER) (2011). Positive thinking: Reduce stress by eliminating negative self-talk. Retrieved May 28, 2011, http://www. mayoclinic.com/health/positive-thinking/SR00009.

McDonald, L. (2006). *Neurons to neighborhoods.* Wisconsin Center for Education Research.

Miller, R., L., Brickman, P., & Bolen, D.(1975) Attribution versus persuasion as a means for modifying behavior. *Journal of Personality and Social Psychology,* 430-441.

Office of Juvenile Justice and Deliquency Prevention. (2010). *Statistical briefing book.*

Parker, B. (2000). *Einstein's brainchild: Relativity made relatively easy!* Amherst: Prometheus Books.

Rosenfeld, L. B., Richman, J. M., & Bowen, G. L. (1998). Low social support among at-risk adolescents. *Social Work in Education, 20*:245-260.

Resnick, M. D., Bearman, P. S., Blum, R. W., Bauman, K. E., Harris, K. M., Jones, J., et al. (1997). Protecting adolescents from harm: Findings from the National Longitudinal Study on Adolescent Health. *JAMA, 278*(10):823-832

Rosenthal, R., & Jacobson, L. (1968). *Pygmalion in the classroom: teacher expectation and pupils' intellectual development.* Norwalk, CT: Crown House Publishing.

Rosenthal, R., & Jacobson, L. (1992). *Pygmalion in the classroom* (Expanded ed.). New York: Irvington.

Rufus, A. (2010, December 23) Mental Time Travel: How does the brain zip back and forth in time? Retrieved November 1, 2011 from *Psychology Today,* http://www.psychologytoday. com/blog/stuck/201012/mental-time-travel

Schwartz, J. (1979). *Einstein for beginners.* New York: Pantheon.

Seligman, M. (1990). *Learned optimism.* New York: AA Knopf.

Sharma, R., & Tripathi, R. C. (1988). Teacher's Expectations and Attributions: The Self-Fulfilling Prophecy Cycle. *Attribution Theory and Research.* New Delhi: Wiley Eastern Limited.

Snyder, C. R. (2000). The Past and Possible Future of Hope. *Journal of Social and Clinical Psychology, 19,* pp. 11-28.

Sociology Guide. (2011). *Culture.* Retrieved Decmber 15, 2011 from http://www.sociologyguide.com/basic-concepts/Culture.php.

The Lineage Project. (2006). An interview with James Gabarino. Retrieved October 20, 2010 f http://www.lineageproject.org/resources02.htm

West, Ed. (2004) *Resilience: A Universal Capacity.* Retrieved from www.wested.org/online_pubs/resiliency/resiliency.chap1.pdf

About the Author

Rick Miller has spent 45 years educating, advocating, caring, and supporting the futures of all youth.

Beginning in 1993, Rick led a seven-year research literature review to better understand the dynamics that lead to success or failure. His findings have revolutionized the understanding of child and youth development.

His breadth of understanding from a research, academic, and practitioner's perspective establishes his credentials as one of most informed and effective spokespersons for children. He is able to translate complicated theory into straightforward and powerful expressions about what is best for youth.

Rick received Arizona State University's Visionary Award in 2007, the Freedoms Foundation at Valley Forge, George Washington Honor Medal in 2009, and the Martin Luther King, Jr. Living the Dream Award from the City of Phoenix, AZ in 2011.

Rick has published several books including *Kids at Hope: Every Child Can Succeed, No Exceptions,* now in its third edition and *Youth Development: From the Trenches A Practitioner Examines the Research, his Experiences, and Discovers a Powerful New Youth Development Strategy.*

Rick served in the White House as a loaned executive during the 1980s in support of the President's Task Force on Private Sector Initiatives. He has also testified before Congress on issues affecting children and youth.

In addition to serving as founder and president of Kids at Hope, an international initiative, Rick also teaches part time at Arizona State University. He is also the Dean of the International Youth Development Master's Institute. In 2000 he was asked to serve as executive director of the City of Phoenix's Violence Prevention Initiative.

Rick crosses over all disciplines and is highly sought as a keynote speaker and presenter to academic, education, recreation, youth development, and law enforcement audiences. His wit, humor, and story-telling abilities captivate the imagination leaving everyone who hears him believing that all children are truly capable of success—no exceptions!

Rick is a husband, father, and grandfather. He lives in Phoenix, Arizona.